FIFTY CLASSIC WALKS IN LANCASHIRE

Terry Marsh

Published by Sigma Leisure – an imprint of
Sigma Press, 1 South Oak Lane, Wilmslow, Cheshire SK9 6AR, England.

British Library Cataloguing in Publication Data
A CIP record for this book is available from the British Library.

ISBN: 1-85058-496-6

Typesetting and Design by: Sigma Press, Wilmslow, Cheshire.

Cover photograph: Drinkwaters Farm, Great Hill, West Pennine Moors
(Terry Marsh)

Cover design: The Agency, Wilmslow

Maps and photographs: Terry Marsh

Printed by: MFP Design and Print

Disclaimer: the information in this book is given in good faith and is believed to be correct at the time of publication. No responsibility is accepted by either the author or publisher for errors or omissions, or for any loss or injury howsoever caused. Only you can judge your own fitness, competence and experience.

Contents

Introduction   1
  Geology   2
  The beginnings of Lancashire   3
  Flora and Fauna   4
  For the purposes of this book . . .   5

The Walks

Walk 1: Arnside and Arnside Knott   16
           Distance: 6 miles (10km)

Walk 2: Leighton Moss and Silverdale   20
           Distance: 5½ miles (9km)

Walk 3: The Four Rivers   25
           Distance: 10 miles (16km)

Walk 4: Green Hill   30
           Distance: 7¼ miles (12km)

Walk 5: Upper Lonsdale   33
           Distance: 6 miles (10km)

Walk 6: Lancaster to Glasson Dock   36
           Distance: 12 miles (19km)

Walk 7: The Lune Valley   **40**
Distance: 16½ miles (26km)

Walk 8: Cockersand Abbey   **46**
Distance: 8¾ miles (14km)

Walk 9: Littledale   **50**
Distance: 5 miles (8km)

Walk 10: Garstang and the Lancaster Canal   **53**
Distance: 7 miles (11km)

Walk 11: Langden Round   **57**
Distance: 5½ miles (9km)

Walk 12: Ward's Stone   **61**
Distance: 18½ km (11½ miles)

Walk 13: Clougha Pike   **64**
Distance: 3½ miles (6km). Variant: 6 miles (10km)

Walk 14: Saddle Fell and Bleadale Water   **68**
Distance: 10 miles (16km)

Walk 15: Parlick and Fair Snape Fell   **72**
Distance: 7½ miles (12km)

Walk 16: Whitendale and Croasdale   **76**
Distance: 12 miles (13km)

Walk 17: Stocks Reservoir Circuit   **79**
Distance: 9 miles (14.5km)

Walk 18: Slaidburn and the River Hodder   **83**
Distance: 7 miles (12km)

Walk 19: Dunsop Head and Whitendale   **87**
Distance: 10 miles (16km)

Walk 20: Nicky Nook and Grize Dale   **90**
Distance: 6 miles (9.5km)

Walk 21: Beacon Fell and the River Brock   **93**
Distance: 7 miles (12km)

Walk 22: Along the Ribble from Ribchester   **97**
Distance: 5 miles (8km)

Walk 23: Longridge Fell   **100**
Distance: 6¼ miles (10km)

Walk 24: Pendle Hill from the Nick of Pendle   **103**
Distance: 6½ miles (10.5km)

Walk 25: Spence Moor   **106**
Distance: 5 miles (8km)

Walk 26: Weets Hill   **112**
Distance: 9 miles (14.5km)

Walk 27: Pendle Hill from Downham   **115**
Distance: 5½ miles (9km)

Walk 28: Pendle Hill Circuit   **118**
Distance: 7 miles (11km)

Walk 29: Wiswell Moor   121
Distance: 6¼ miles (10km)

Walk 30: Formby and Ainsdale Dunes   125
Distance: 3½ miles (6km)

Walk 31: Rufford and Croston   128
Distance: 12½ miles (20.5km)

Walk 32: The Rainford Loop   133
Distance: 6 miles (10km)

Walk 33: Ashurst Beacon and Beacon Country Park   136
Distance: 3 miles (5km)

Walk 34: Cuerden Valley and the River Lostock   140
Distance: 5½ miles (9km)

Walk 35: Wigan Pier to Haigh Country Park   145
Distance: 5½ miles (9km) [or 9 miles (15km)]

Walk 36: Around Pennington Flash   150
Distance: 3 miles (5km)

Walk 37: The Bold Loop   153
Distance: 9 miles (14km)

Walk 38: Boulsworth Hill   156
Distance: 8 miles (13km)

Walk 39: Black Hameldon   160
Distance: 8½ miles (14km)

Walk 40: Thieveley Pike and Black Scout   163
Distance: 7 miles (11km)

Walk 41: Blackstone Edge   166
Distance: 6¼ miles (10km)

Walk 42: Saddleworth Edges   170
Distance: 8 miles (13km)

Walk 43: Around Pleasington   175
Distance: 6 miles (10km)

Walk 44: Darwen Moor West   180
Distance: 8 miles (12.5km)

Walk 45: Jumbles and Wayoh Reservoirs   185
Distance: 6 miles (10km)

Walk 46: Rivington to White Coppice via the Woodland Trail 189
Distance: 8 miles (13km)

Walk 47: Great Hill and Spitler's Edge from White Coppice 193
Distance: 7 miles (12km)

Walk 48: Darwen Moor   197
Distance: 10 miles (16km)

Walk 49: Winter Hill and Lever Park   201
Distance: 9 miles (14.5km)

Walk 50: Bull Hill and the Peel Monument   207
Distance: 4½ miles (7.5km)

Bibliography   211

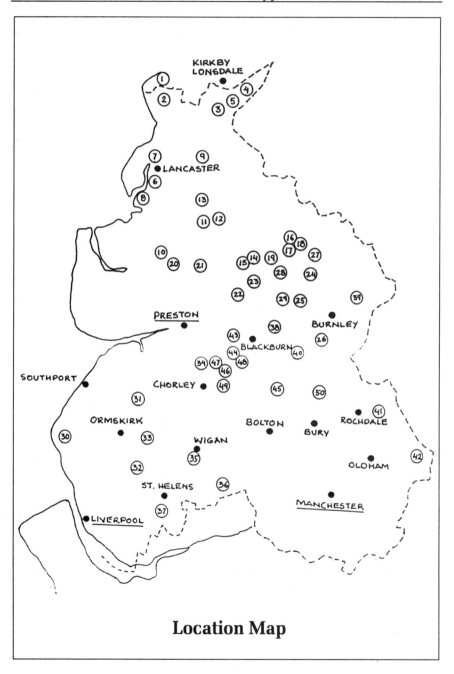

Location Map

Introduction

In the Foreword to his book on Lancashire, the late and much-missed comedian Les Dawson commented that the county is "many things to many people", conjuring up for some images of "vast smoky grey blocks of heavy industry", while to others Lancashire is a "memory of lakes and woods and rolling hills". Few, I suspect, will instantly identify with the latter, yet Lancashire boasts two sizeable areas that have been designated as Areas of Outstanding Natural Beauty. The larger is the Forest of Bowland, with an area of 310 square miles (800 sq km), while the other, much smaller at 29 square miles (75 sq km), is the Arnside and Silverdale AONB.

If nothing else, this book sets out to show that there is much less smoky greyness about modern Lancashire, and considerably more from which to fashion fond memories. Those, like me, who were born and bred in the county have known the truth for a long time, so I take not inconsiderable pleasure from being in a position to let others in on the secrets of Lancashire, the Red Rose county.

But where is Lancashire? Whither the Red Rose? Over the years the boundaries have been so frequently changed that it is difficult to decide what is, or isn't, Lancashire. So, some arbitrary decision-making has been necessary. Merseyside and Greater Manchester, as metropolitan county councils, have long since disappeared, and their component parts have metamorphosed into unitary authorities, not a lot different from what they were pre-1974, when the last major reshuffle took place. A good deal of this area always was Lancashire, and many folk who live there still think of it as Lancashire, as I do, but then I was born in the middle of it, and no desk-bound mandarin with an itchy felt-tip marker is going to deny me my birthright.

It is, too, a source of irritation that not only did Lancashire lose Furness, Lancashire-over-the-Sands as it was known, to Cumbria, but also that the northern boundary of Lancashire at this point could not be pushed out into the Kent Estuary, which would have made a logical dividing line. But Arnside and its delightful countryside used to be in Westmorland, not Lancashire, so I can see why it was lumped in with Cumbria, however illogical it still seems. Anyway, I've ignored that little distinction, and included Arnside in this book, but I have conceded that Furness is forever gone. At the southern end of the county, the River Mersey ceased to be the boundary between Lancashire and Cheshire, while along the county's eastern flank the boundary reached out and stole the Forest of Bowland from Yorkshire, but we always felt it was ours anyway!

Geology

The most significant period of geological evolution for Lancashire occurred about 350 million years ago when Britain was covered by water and Carboniferous beds of limestone were laid down. Limestone from this time can be found around Clitheroe. Gradually this covering of limestone thickened, but also became overlaid with river deposits which then hardened into Millstone Grit which aeons later supplied the stone from which many of the buildings of the county were built. As the river deposits spread ever more widely, the covering water became very shallow in places, so much so that swamp-like vegetation emerged.

Some 250 million years ago, the limestone underwent considerable folding, and this was followed by erosion which removed, for example, the summits of the limestone regions of what is now Bowland and Rossendale. But whatever went on in these distant times, it was radically changed by the Ice Ages that followed. The ice sheet layered boulder clay and sand in the valleys and diverted streams. As the glaciers retreated, they left behind a series of lakes that later, having drained, were to prove to be important channels of communication between neighbouring valleys. A good example of this is found at Cliviger, between Todmorden and Burnley (Walk 40).

Subsequent alluvial deposits and the evolution of peat mosses were the last two important geological events in Lancashire prehistory. The alluvial deposits formed the West Lancashire Plain and the mudflats of the Fylde, while the peat mosses, evidence of which can still be seen in the walk around Rufford and Croston (Walk 31), were used for fuel. The peatbogs were then drained, mostly in the last two hundred years.

After the last Ice Age, which is thought to have ended about 11 000 to 10 000 years ago, the climate in Britain became significantly warmer, encouraging the widespread growth of oak and birch. These forests, which covered all but the highest ground of the county, provided shelter and resources for the first human settlers, who are thought to have arrived in the Lancashire region about 7 000 years ago. Many parts of the West Pennine Moors bear evidence of the presence of early man, who, along with the Scandinavian invaders who settled in the area much later, was responsible for clearing much of the forest domain.

The beginnings of Lancashire

The ancient county of Lancashire came into being during the reign of Henry II (1154-89), when the first sheriff was appointed to collect taxes for the whole county. The earldom of Lancaster was invented for Henry III's youngest son, Edmund Crouchback, in 1266, and he was given extensive powers within the county. In 1351, when the fourth earl, Henry, was awarded the title of duke, he was granted palatine powers for life by Edward III. This authority gave Henry a position not unlike that of the Earl of Chester and the Bishop of Durham, and vested in him the right to exercise immense powers in matters such as the appointment of judges and the holding of courts. When Henry died the palatine powers were resumed by the king, but were later granted to his successor, John of Gaunt, 29 years later. When he died, the duchy was seized by his nephew, Richard II, whereupon Gaunt's son, Henry Bolingbroke, returned from exile and recovered both duchy and kingdom from his cousin, and was crowned Henry IV, the first of the royal house of Lancaster. The duchy was never again surrendered by the reigning monarch, and the Loyal Toast in Lancashire is to "The Queen, Duke of Lancaster".

The first occasion on which the 'county' of Lancaster appears was in 1168. The town's principal advantage lay in its strategic position in relation to the Lune valley, a main through route to Scotland. But this command diminished as the military significance of its castle declined and as other important centres to the south grew. In 1798 the seat of county government switched from Lancaster to Preston, where it has remained ever since.

Flora and Fauna

In an era when, at last, we are becoming aware of the threat to our environment, it is encouraging to see how positively the powers that be in Lancashire have responded by protecting much of our flora and fauna and the landscape they inhabit, and in some cases even improving on what was there before. To develop public awareness of the issues the county council has developed a Landscape and Wildlife Strategy, and works in close partnership with agencies like North West Water, the Royal Society for the Protection of Birds, the Wetlands Trust, the Lancashire Wildlife Trust and the Woodland Trust, along with many others.

For wildlife to succeed, their habitats must remain intact, and though motorways often plough uncaringly through nature reserves, it is by the development of nature reserves that many habitats can be afforded some protection. But for nature reserves to be marooned in the middle of a network of roads without vital wildlife corridor links does not give the degree of protection we might think. Fragmentation of habitat sites is as much a problem as no protection at all, and has the effect of reducing genetic diversity so that in the long term many species will die out, even in a nature reserve. The issues are complex, but if each of us gains a token understanding of the problems, then we may ultimately build the causeways needed to bridge the difficulties. Sadly, what is lost, is lost. Nevertheless, it is important that by showing an awareness of and active support for the many issues involved, we at least slow the pace at which the natural beauty of our countryside is destroyed, even if we cannot altogether halt it.

Lancashire can boast a very wide range of habitat: from upland moors where grouse breed and sparrowhawks and kestrel hunt, to coastal marshes and inland meres that provide a haven for bittern, bearded tit, hen and marsh harriers. Between the two, woodland and scrub areas provide shelter for woodcock, snipe, owls, woodpeckers and a staggering range of smaller birds. Leighton Moss Reserve near Silverdale records more than 200 species of birds, and an impressive listing of mammals, butterflies and wild flowers. Pennington Flash almost annually attracts national and local rarities including spoonbill, ring-billed gulls, Slavonian grebes, little ringed plovers and green sandpipers. Elsewhere you can expect to find fallow, red and roe deer, as well as occasional sightings of sika deer, which were introduced into Britain in the nineteenth century.

Much of the change to the Lancashire landscape is due to a combination of expanding residential development, i.e. bad planning, and farming methods that have meant the ripping out of miles of hedgerows (something like 150 000 miles of hedgerow have been lost in this way throughout Britain since the last war), the draining of peatland mosses (only 1 per cent of the peatmoss land that existed in Lancashire in the seventeenth century now remains), the destruction of traditional hay meadows, and the spread of glaring yellow fields of oilseed rape. The changes in farming methods have taken a heavy toll of Lancashire's wild flowers, mainly due to the widespread use of artificial fertilisers. Since wild flowers are a vital part of the ecosystems of many creatures, insects for example, which in turn form part of the survival needs for other animals, the loss of wild flower areas is a major concern.

Thankfully, many areas remain to provide a wealth of flora and fauna from the mudflats of Morecambe Bay and the Ribble estuary, to the reserves and country parks of Leighton Moss, Martin Mere, Pennington Flash, Cuerden Valley Park, Stocks Reservoir, and many more.

For the purposes of this book . . .

I have divided the county into seven areas, though the distinction is purely organisational from my point of view, and should not be taken seriously. The areas are Arnside and Silverdale; Lonsdale and the Fylde Coast; the Forest of Bowland; Pendleside and the Ribble

Valley; Central and Southern Lancashire; the South Pennines; and the West Pennine Moors.

Within these areas there is another self-contained area known these days as Lancashire's Hill Country. This modern manifestation comprises Blackburn, Burnley, Hyndburn and Rossendale, and is an area rich in upland countryside, industrial heritage and fascinating villages and towns. Further west, many of the villages of Lancashire's coastal plain are among the oldest in the country, and prove to be perfect springboards from which to launch into an exploration of a flatter, but ornithologically fascinating, area of the county.

Arnside and Silverdale

The area around Arnside and Silverdale on the Kent Estuary is certainly one of the most secluded and delightful places in the county, where wooded limestone hills shelter attractive villages, and the landscape proves to be an amazing place of wildlife wonder, hosting an enormous range of bird life and flora.

Almost half of the area is woodland, mainly broadleaved (and a surprising number of yews). But there are large expanses of estuarial marshlands and salt flats, limestone pavement and heathland. Such diversity has meant that Arnside and Silverdale have become an Area of Outstanding Natural Beauty (AONB). These areas differ from national parks in the way they are administered, and their main function is to encourage land use which will promote conservation and maintain the landscape, as well as providing a degree of protection against inappropriate planning developments.

Lonsdale and the Fylde Coast

The River Lune rises among the north-eastern fells of the Howgills, in Cumbria, and carves its way through the hills, in so doing providing a long-standing through route to Scotland, before swinging westwards to reach the sea near Lancaster. To the south of this, and north of the Ribble at Preston lies the ancient Hundred of Amounderness, now known as the Fylde coast. Seen from afar this coastal plain seems like a flat, featureless expanse, but closer inspection reveals considerable diversity.

The Lune itself provides excellent walking opportunities, and because of its strategic importance in medieval times, the towns and villages along its banks are heavy with the history of Lancashire and of England.

The Forest of Bowland

The Forest of Bowland and Pendle Hill were designated as Areas of Outstanding Natural Beauty in 1964, and though Pendle Hill is quite separate geographically, the two together share the title Forest of Bowland AONB. It is the eleventh largest of the 40 designated AONBs and is almost entirely in Lancashire, though a small area extends into Yorkshire.

The forest is, of course, a former hunting forest, not a woodland, while the name 'Bowland' probably derives from 'bu'-land, the land of cattle, and has nothing to do with bows and arrows. In times gone by wild boar, deer and wolves roamed here, making the area a much-prized hunting ground for kings and nobility.

The central core of the area contrasts gritstone fells with steep-sided valleys and peaty moorland expanses, and for many years access to this excellent walking country was a vexed subject. Gradually, however, the diligent and careful efforts of the county council's countryside service are beginning to develop areas of open access and agreed routes across the fells, that make the exploration of Bowland a much easier, and more lawful, proposition.

Pendleside and the Ribble Valley

Pendle will forever be linked with tales of witchcraft, indeed, it was once said that witches even filled the burrows alongside the rabbits, so numerous were they. Certainly the myths and legends that grew up around these claims prompted an excellent book by Harrison Ainsworth, *The Lancashire Witches*, that makes ideal supplementary reading for anyone coming to this region for the first time.

The River Ribble, for the most part a majestic river, rises far away in the Yorkshire Dales, on the slopes of Whernside, one of the Three Peaks of Yorkshire, but it is not long before it becomes Lancashire's river, and flows through idyllic countryside, into Pendle, on by

Ribchester, where the Romans had a fort, and on to meet the sea near Preston.

Central and Southern Lancashire

This amorphous grouping effectively mops up what is not contained in the other areas I have described. It embraces the coastal scenery near Southport, and reaches inland, into what is technically Merseyside, to explore the countryside around Rainford and Bold, both ancient family strongholds in the former county of Lancashire. On the way it visits historic houses, ancient beacon sites, and centres of considerable wildlife interest, from squirrel sanctuaries at Formby, to ornithological sites like Pennington Flash at Leigh and Haigh Country Park, near Wigan.

This is a region of the county that holds its own fascinations, where the walking is less arduous but equally as rewarding as the heights of the Forest of Bowland or the West Pennine Moors, and where you are sure to spend many happy hours wandering its country lanes and by-ways.

The South Pennines

The full area of the South Pennines straddles both Lancashire and Yorkshire and extends northwards to touch upon the Yorkshire Dales, and southwards to the edge of the Peak National Park. For the purposes of this book, a much smaller area has been used, one that might just as easily be called East Lancashire. Here the county meets up with Yorkshire and Greater Manchester and provides walkers with a multitude of fine treks that explore a landscape where history shrieks at you from every new turn in the trail. Here you find evidence of the occupation of the Romans, there the sad desolation of derelict, lonely farmsteads high on the moors, while the whole area is criss-crossed with ingrained trails trodden by packhorse trains and dotted with the relics of the milling industries that flourished here.

Here, among what my colleague John Gillham calls the 'Cloth Cap Hills', beauty is never far distant, and is to be found in the most unexpected places.

The West Pennine Moors

Buttressed by the towns of Bolton and Bury, Blackburn, Chorley, Accrington and Haslingden, the West Pennine Moors enjoy a justly-deserved popularity. That popularity was hard won: as long ago as 1896, the people of Bolton and Darwen marched on to the moors in protest, to fight for rights of access that now, a hundred years on, remain no less popular, and no less important. Indeed, amid calls for the freedom to roam to be recognised as a fundamental human right under European Law, that right already exists on the West Pennine Moors, if only as a result of negotiated access agreements under which walkers can strike out across the moors to experience the freedom of open country. Many of the access agreements have been in place since the 1950s, but all of them were renewed in the mid-1990s. Only the western part of the moors, however, offers such freedom of access, and much more remains to be done, especially in the east.

The Moors cover 90 square miles of upland, valleys, farmland and reservoirs, and can be as bleak and inhospitable as any moorland tract in Britain.

Farming has always been important on the moors, in spite of a harsh climate and poor, acidic soil that supports sparse grasses on which sheep and cattle graze. Not surprisingly, farmers often found it necessary to take on other work to support their families, and many worked at quarrying sandstone for buildings, pavements, walls and millstones for grinding corn. If you inspect the walls on the moors you will find how suitable the coarse-grained millstone grit was for producing the great circles of stone with which to grind corn.

Yet, in spite of dramatic changes in the industrial profile of the surrounding towns, the West Pennine Moors remain a working landscape, with farming once more a dominant land use. Most of the quarries that supplied the stone are now derelict, save for the opportunities they offer the rock-climbing fraternity; all that exists to tell of the coal mining industry are a few scattered spoil heaps and isolated mine shafts, but in the valleys the land has been improved, pastures rejuvenated, and some areas afforested to meet a local and wider need for timber.

And, as if resuming a mantle it never quite shed, the area once more serves man's recreational needs, providing a valuable oasis of escapism for those who care not to venture to the over-crowded honeypots of the Lake District, the Peak and the Yorkshire Dales.

It is a fitting tribute that the West Pennine Moors form a focal point for many people of south Lancashire, but the attraction of the landscape has generated for this traditional recreational area all the problems, on a lesser scale, experienced in the national parks. Without proper and considerate management, the Moors would suffer irreparable damage to what is essentially a major water catchment area.

Probably the greatest centre of activity is the mini-Lakeland around the Anglezarke and Rivington reservoirs on the south-western edge of the Moors. Man has lived in this area from Bronze Age times, while the very place names indicate a Scandinavian influence. For several centuries Rivington was in the hands of the Pilkington family, having been purchased from the de Rivington family more than 700 years ago. In the 1600s, the estate was sold to Robert Lever and Thomas Breres. A hundred years later it passed into the sole ownership of John Andrews, with whose family the manorial rights remained until sold in 1900 to William Hesketh Lever, who created Lever Park and the Terraced Gardens that flank the slopes of Rivington Pike. The area of Anglezarke has had a much less chequered ownership, having remained in the ownership of the Standish family since the late 1600s. Both estates subsequently became the property of Liverpool Corporation, which bought them to develop a water supply for the conurbation. In 1974, they became the responsibility of North West Water.

Such is the variety of interest and opportunity for relaxation and recreation in the West Pennine Moors, that many days of exploration will be necessary to do it all justice.

Notes and Advice for Walkers

None of the walks suggested in this book presents technical problems in good weather conditions, especially in summer. The vast majority may also be tackled in winter by competent walkers. Some of the walks traverse bleak and featureless moorland where mist becomes a major hazard.

For all the walks I have assumed that readers possess navigational skills, are conversant with map and compass technique, and know how to clothe and protect themselves effectively. In winter, with snow and ice on the ground, an ice-axe is an essential item of equipment on some walks, but it is useless without the knowledge to use it properly. And there may be times and places when crampons will greatly facilitate progress.

Maps: Each walk carries details of the most appropriate Ordnance Survey map(s), and is supported by a diagrammatic map outlining the walk. The diagrammatic map is not sufficient for use in lieu of an Ordnance Survey map.

Various maps covering Lancashire are available to the walker, all are produced by Ordnance Survey. These are:

Landranger Maps are produced to a scale of 1:50 000 (1¼ inches to 1 mile or 2cm to 1km), and are all-purpose maps. Landranger maps, of which 204 are required for the whole country, each cover an area 25 x 25 miles (40 x 40km), i.e. 625 square miles (1600 square kilometres). All Landranger maps contain Rights of Way information, such as footpaths and bridleways, and the maps are available in both flat and folded form, the latter proving a handy size to carry in pockets or rucksacks.

Outdoor Leisure Maps cover popular leisure and recreation areas of the country, and are packed with detail invaluable to the serious walker. They are to a scale of 1:25 000 (2½ inches to 1 mile or 4cm to 1km). In 1996 a new OLM was introduced which covers the Forest of Bowland and Ribblesdale; in addition you will need the sheet for the South Pennines and that for the Yorkshire Dales Western area.

Pathfinder Maps are also to a scale of 1:25 000, and since 1989 cover the entire country. There are 1373 in total, most covering an area 20km east to west and 10km north to south. Where the area of a Pathfinder Map is completely covered by an Outdoor Leisure Map, then the Pathfinder Map may not be available.

During the currency of this book, all the Pathfinder maps produced by Ordnance Survey will be replaced by the new Explorer series. One of the first of these, number 19, covers the West Pennine Moors, and is especially useful. This will be renumbered in time, as the complete new system develops.

Distances and *Height gain* are approximate and have been rounded up or down, but they are sufficiently accurate to allow calculation of times using Naismith's or other rules.

Walking times are my estimate of how long the walk should take an averagely fit person. The times make no allowance for stops of any kind.

Paths: There are numerous paths throughout Lancashire's countryside, indeed the county is well stocked with rights of way, but it should be noted that *any reference to paths or other lines of ascent does not imply that a right of way exists.*

Access: The author has walked without challenge throughout the Lancashire countryside for many years, and most walkers will enjoy the same liberty. This general freedom, achieved and maintained only by considerate walkers, should not be interpreted as a licence to clamber over walls and fences indiscriminately causing damage, or to tramp through fields of crops. To travel anywhere on the hills and moors with a dog that is not held on a leash is inviting the justifiable wrath of those who own the land and earn a living from it.

Gear for walking: At certain times of the year some parts of every walk in this book are affected by rain, becoming muddy or peaty. For this reason proper footwear in the form of leather boots is recommended; canvas and suede boots, especially the modern lightweight boots, are, however, more than adequate most of the time, but cannot cope with the worst conditions. For these times and conditions a spare pair of socks or two in your rucksack will mean you can change to dry footwear, if necessary.

Flashy walking breeches, as such, are not needed. Any warm trousers capable of withstanding wind and (some) rain are ideal, but not jeans, which are too restrictive, very uncomfortable when wet and take a long time to dry. The modern lightweight trousers made specifically for outdoor use are excellent, and tougher than they look.

Upper body inner clothing which supports the layer principle of insulation need not be the pricey garments found in equipment shops. Very often a couple of old sweaters serve just as well, but it is important to have a good quality outer garment, windproof and waterproof, for both the upper and lower body, and of that there is a vast array. My maxim has always been to find the most expensive garment I can afford, and then buy something a little more expensive – investment in good quality mountain clothing saves lives! It is essential to maintain an even body temperature; this may be affected by damp and cold and could lead to hypothermia, a serious and potentially fatal condition. Up to twenty per cent of body heat loss escapes via the head, so it is a good idea to wear a cap or balaclava, no matter how daft you think you look.

All the walks in this book may be easily accommodated within a few hours, but time enough to justify a daysack to carry drinks and food, spare clothing, emergency rations, first aid kit, a torch, whistle, map and compass.

Public transport

It would be foolhardy to suggest we should abolish motor cars, they are too convenient. But a car's acid emission does nothing for the very things we love in the countryside. One of the things we can do to help is to use public transport whenever we are going out for a walk. Buses are more environmentally friendly than cars, and trains more than buses.

All the walks in this book can be undertaken using public transport; a few can only be done at very limited times, during the summer months, and some will mean adding to the walking distance in order to get from the nearest point to which public transport operates to the start of the walk.

At the beginning of each walk I have listed the form and operators of public transport services. Under 'Rail' I have given the nearest railway station. Information about rail services in any part of the county can be obtained by ringing National Rail Enquiries on 0345 484950. Under 'Bus' I have given a code for bus service operators. Information about bus services to and from Lancashire can be obtained by ringing the Train, Bus and Coach Hotline on 0891 910910. Within the county, the following coded table will furnish you with up-to-date information about services.

Code	Operator	Address	Telephone
ABT	ABC Travel	7 Rothwell Drive, Ainsdale, Southport PT8 2SB	01704 576033
AOR	AOR Travel	Railway Buildings, Station Yard, Midge Hall Lane, Leyland PR5 3TM	01772 622240
BBT	Blackburn Borough Transport	Intack Garage, Whitebirk Road, Blackburn BB1 3JD	01254 51112
BOR	Border	Heasandford Villa, Burnley BB10 2AH	01282 456351
BPT	Burnley and Pendle Transport	Queensgate, Colne Road, Burnley BB10 1HH	01282 425244
CSV	Crosville	Woodhouse Street, Stoke-on-Trent ST4 1EQ	01244 315400
DCS	Darwen Coach Services	5 West View, Knowle Lane, Chapels, Darwen BB3 0EG	01254 776877
ELM	East Lancashire Motors	Whalley Road, Langho, Blackburn BB6 8EQ	01254 238808
FWK	J Fishwick and Sons	Golden Hill Garage, Leyland PR5 2LE	01772 421207
GMB	GM Buses North	Wallshaw Street, Oldham OL1 3TR	0161 627 2929
HOR	New Horizons	1 Glencarron Close, Hoddlesden, Darwen BB3 3RF	01254 776622
HYN	Hyndburn Borough Transport	140a Blackburn Road, Accrington BB5 0AD	01254 390816
KIL	Kirkby Lonsdale Mini Coaches	Twenty Acres, Moor End, Hutton Roof, Carnforth LA6 2PF	015242 72239
LAK	Lakelands	Westview, The Dene, Hurst Green, Nr Clitheroe BB7 9QF	01254 826646
MPT	Merseybus	Green Lane, Stoneycroft, Liverpool L13 7HS	0151 254 1254
NWR	North Western Road Car Co	73 Ormskirk Road, Aintree, Liverpool L9 5AE	0151 525 1733
PEN	Pennine Motor Services	Grouse Garage, Gargrave, Skipton BD23 3RB	01756 749215
RIB	Stagecoach Ribble	Frenchwood Avenue, Preston PR1 4LU	01772 886633
TCH	Town Car Hire	Victoria Street Garage, Victoria Street, Clitheroe BB7 1BL	01200 443322
WLC	White Lady Coaches	1 Glencarropn Close, Hoddlesden, Darwen BB3 3RF	01254 771893
YOR	Calderline	Skircoat Road, Halifax HX1 2RF	01422 365985

In addition there are a number of Leisure Link Bus services operated on behalf of the county council. These run on Sundays and Bank Holidays from May until September. These are:

Service 40: Bowland Rambler: Colne – Burnley – Morecambe – Arnside – Grange-over-Sands, via Litheroe and Trough of Bowland
Service 40: Morecambe Rambler: Morecambe – Silverdale – Arnside – Grange-over-Sands
Service 43: Ribble Valley Rambler: Skelmersdale – Ormskirk – Preston – Clitheroe – Slaidburn – Settle
Service 44: Bowland Pathfinder: Preston – Beacon Fell – Dunsop Bridge – Slaidburn – Clitheroe

Service 45: Bowland Rambler: Darwen – Blackburn – Accrington – Morecambe, via Clitheroe and Trough of Bowland
Service 70/71: Pendle Witch Hopper: Burnley – Sabden – Clitheroe – Downham – Barley – Nelson – Burnley

You can get information about these Leisure Link Services, and all other bus services in Lancashire, by ringing one of the County Information Centres:

Accrington:	01254 872595
Blackburn:	01254 681120
Blackpool:	01253 751485
Burnley:	01282 423125
Charnock Richard:	01257 793773
Chorley:	01257 241693
Clitheroe:	01200 442226
Fleetwood:	01253 772704
Lancaster:	01524 841656
Leyland:	01772 621857
Lytham:	01253 794405
Morecambe:	01524 582808
Nelson:	01282 698533
Ormskirk:	01695 579062
Preston:	01772 556618
Rawtenstall:	01706 213677
Skelmersdale:	01695 50463

Walk 1: Arnside and Arnside Knott

Start/Finish: Arnside. GR.455787

Distance: 6 miles (10km)

Height gain: 640ft (195m)

Walking time: 3-4 hours

Type of Walk: Generally easy, with two small ascents. Often blustery along the coastal section.

Map: OS Pathfinder 636: Grange-over-Sands.

Public transport: *Rail:* Arnside. *Bus:* Leisure Link 40 (Bowland and Morecambe Ramblers) to Arnside (Sundays and Bank Holidays from May-September only).

Not Such a Knotty Problem

Quite what the powers that be were thinking when they lumped Arnside in with Cumbria, when there is a perfectly good county boundary in the form of the Kent Estuary close by, is beyond me. But I have no intention of allowing this administrative idiosyncrasy to prevent me from including this delightful walk around the Kent coastline and over Arnside Knott, part of which does go into Lancashire; it is one of the outstanding walks in this region, and justly popular.

In a sense, Arnside is an illogical start to a walk because it is just the sort of place where sitting, watching and listening impose equal demands on your time. What you will watch, mostly, are the birds that frequent the estuary and the intrepid walkers who set off to cross Morecambe Bay in the company of official sand pilot, Cedric Robinson (to attempt this without a guide or considerable local knowledge of the sands, is folly in the extreme). The birds are many in number, the hopefuls rather fewer.

Here goosanders patrol the murky, silt-laden Kent in advance of

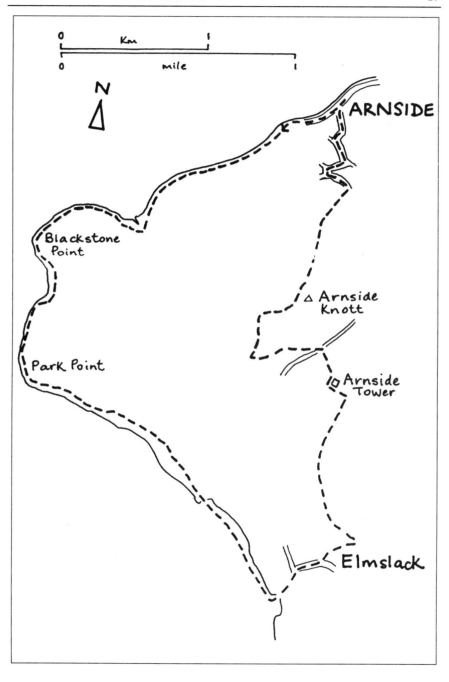

the incoming tide, while oystercatchers, curlews, redshanks, sand-pipers and tiny sanderlings fuss about at the water's edge. And there are the independent sentinels, too, a poised grey heron, intent on its own business, and the occasional buzzard that floats across the wooded slopes of Arnside Knott.

Along the shore fishermen cast their lines, hoping to catch fluke or flounders, though how many of these flat-fish species still remain in the bay is debatable. Among the watchers, older residents of the village may be encouraged to talk of the days when Arnside had a thriving coastal trade, when boat-building sheds proliferated, and Arnside had its own Customs House. The coming of the railway in 1849, thrusting its long viaduct across the Kent where an old ford used to be principal way across the Milnthorpe Sands, brought an end to this.

Arnside used to belong to the Manor and Township of Beetham, and the earliest form of its name was derived from that of a settler, Earnwulf, who quite likely took the prominent headland, Arnul-vesheved, as his base. Old writers have noted how, "Many visitors come hither in summer, the air being remarkably salubrious, and the scenery beautifully diversified and picturesque." The visitors still come, the air is still remarkably invigorating, and the scenery, in spite of man's lack of taste in matters of visual amenity, much as it always has been.

Start along the concrete walkway at the end of the promenade that leads eventually to the shore, continuing past the Coastguard sta-tion, where stretches of bare rock are worth checking for fossils, mainly bits of coral, brachiopods and crinoids. Soon the shore walk leads to a broad bay, cut by a deep creek. Taken head-on, the creek can be awkward to cross, so bear left and walk round it on a clear path, keeping eyes and ears open for the occasional great spotted woodpeckers that frequent the adjacent woodlands.

The route sticks to the coastline, rounding the slight rise of Frith Wood. Before long it arrives at Blackstone Point, where the coast changes direction, turning abruptly southwards. If the tide is in, it may be difficult to keep precisely to the shore line at Blackstone Point, but thankfully you can escape on to a path across the top of nearby cliffs.

Continue around to another bay, White Creek, from where most cross-bay walks now launch themselves, and where a path runs into weather-beaten woodland along the cliff top towards Park Point. The cliff-top path is a delight to follow, but eventually descends to the saltings, wide acres of sea-washed turf spreading across Silverdale Bay. Across the Bay lies Silverdale, and though a direct line across the saltings seems easy enough, you soon realise that the many pools and inlets can involve a lot of casting about. The best way is to parallel the cliffs along the coastal edge.

Keep on until you reach Silverdale Cove, beyond a caravan site, where we leave the coast. Turn left here and follow a lane to reach Elmslack at a road junction and bend. Turn right, heading towards the village for a short distance, and soon take a path slanting on the left to pass between houses to a back lane at the foot of Eaves Wood Nature Reserve, also known as King William's Hill. Turn right and ascend the lane, which soon deteriorates, continuing as a rough track through woodland to emerge in a caravan park. Keeping the caravan site on your left, head right across sparsely-wooded but much-flowered Middlebarrow Plain to reach a stile and gate at the end of a green lane, close by Arnside Tower.

Arnside Tower is a 'pele', or fortified household, dating from the time of the Border Troubles. It was built about 1340, "for the defence of the coasts against the invasions of foreign or domestic enemies", and is said to have been inhabited until 1690, though records suggest it experienced considerable destruction as a result of a "mighty winde" in October 1602, an act of Godly destruction that was completed some years later.

Go past the tower, then through the farmyard beyond to a lane leading up to the road below Arnside Knott, where a National Trust sign directs you onward along Saul's Drive. This is a well-made path that climbs through yew-adorned woods, turning right at a crosspath to reach the highest point. Nothing, but sad relics, now remains of the knotted trees for which Arnside Knott was once famous, but the splendour of its panorama is diminished not one whit.

Keep ahead, roughly north, to descend to meet a wall and stile. Cross this and go down into woodland below, savouring the wide views as you go. Once in the lower woodland a path leads you down to a lane. Turn left, and follow village lanes, ever-descending, into the village.

Walk 2: Leighton Moss and Silverdale

Start/Finish: Silverdale (Leighton Moss). GR.477750

Distance: 5½ miles (9km)

Height gain: Nominal

Walking time: 2-2½ hours

Type of Walk: Generally easy; care needed on road and rail sections. Can be muddy. Some of the squeeze stiles may cause inconvenience for some.

Map: OS Pathfinder 636: Grange-over-Sands

Public transport: *Rail:* Silverdale. *Bus:* RIB and MTL operate to Silverdale.

Leighton Possibilities

Walkers visiting the Silverdale area have a vast network of footpaths and bridleways from which to devise delightful meandering circuits. This is one of the outstanding features of the northern edge of Lancashire, an area that is quite simply exquisite and rich in natural history, especially the bird life that frequents the haunts of Leighton Moss and the adjacent Morecambe Bay sands.

This walk, which visits the Royal Society for the Protection of Birds' reserve at Leighton Moss, Leighton Hall, and the National Trust property at Eaves Wood, amply demonstrates how versatile this superb corner of the county really is. Members of the RSPB can use the car park at Myers Farm Visitor Centre; non-members will find places alongside the road to Yealand Storrs though I dare say that if you plan to visit the RSPB shop and café at some stage, then no one is likely to crib if you use the car park. A more environmentally-friendly alternative is to use one of the bus services that run to Silverdale, or to take the train to the nearby station. Begin along the

Leighton Hall, Silverdale

road, towards Yealand Storrs, to reach the fragmites-flanked public bridleway across Leighton Moss reserve.

Leighton Moss has been an RSPB reserve since 1964, and covers an area of 134 hectares (321 acres). The adjacent Morecambe Bay reserve was bought by the RSPB in 1974 and 1981 and covers 1675 hectares (4140 acres). More than 255 species of birds have been recorded on the reserve, of which 75 breed regularly; more than 532 species of plants have been recorded on the site, along with more than 30 species of butterfly.

Large numbers of wildfowl use the open water area for much of the year, while the elusive and secretive bitterns are the rarest inhabitants of the reedbeds. Water rails, bearded tits and sedge warblers also frequent the reedbeds, while the skies above are patrolled by marsh harriers, sparrowhawks and peregrines.

At the end of the causeway keep ahead through a gate and follow a track curving left to Grisedale Farm. Go past the farm to a surfaced lane leading up to Leighton Hall.

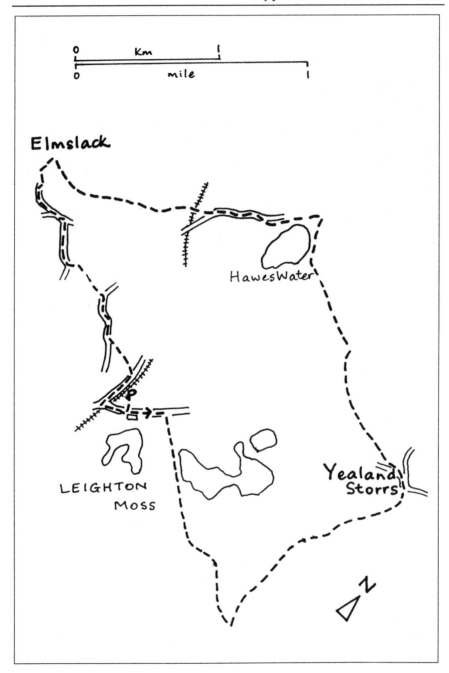

Leighton Hall is still lived in by the Gillow family, of Waring and Gillow furniture manufacturers' fame. It is a beautiful country house, and stands where a house has stood since medieval times. In 1173 land was granted by William de Lancaster to Adam d'Avranches, who constructed a fortified manor not long after. It was re-built in 1760, having been destroyed in 1715 by Government troops returning from chasing Jacobite rebels northwards. In 1786 the estate was sold to a Lancaster banker, Alexander Worswick, whose mother was Alice Gillow, and it was he who was responsible for adding, in 1825, the neo-Gothic façade we see today. The hall is open to the public during summer months only, and it is well worth walking the extra distance to reach it.

Having done so, retrace your steps down the lane to a footpath (signposted Yealand Storrs) near some houses, or, if you have no wish to go to Leighton Hall, simply take to the path as you reach it. This leads across many fields, roughly in a northerly direction, until you pass the access to Brow Foot Farm. Move away from the wall at this point, following a wide track to a small group of cottages at Yealand Storrs. Go through a gate and pass in front of the cottages to a small gate to the right of a much larger one. This brings you out on the road.

Turn left along the road for a short distance to a bend and road junction. Leave the road here, through a gate, and enter the yew-filled plantations of Yealand Hall Allotment. A broad track now runs on for quite some distance. There are numerous lesser side branches, but ignore all of these. At the first main fork, keep left, and at the second, keep right (though it's really still ahead).

Eventually, the track becomes a narrow path running beside a wall, and soon reaches a squeeze stile beside a gate. Through the stile, head slightly right across a field to a ladder stile at an access to English Nature's Gait Barrows Nature Reserve. Keep in the same direction across the next two fields to enter the woodland that adjoins Hawes Water at a stile.

Follow a waymarked track to the right and then stay with it, ignoring any branches, as it curves beside a wall round the top end of the lake finally to emerge on to a road near Challan Hall. Go down the lane, but take care as there are a few blind bends and undulations. Leave the road at a path on the right (signposted Eaves Wood). Follow the path, enclosed by wire fencing, down to another lane. Turn left and then very soon right, to cross the railway line – with care!

Beyond the railway line, keep ahead across a number of driveways to enter the National Trust property of Eaves Wood. Keep ahead into the wood and at the first junction bear left. Then at a fork climb right to meet a broad and more pronounced pathway that will now lead you ahead (yellow waymark). Fork left (another yellow waymark) when the path branches, and keep in the same direction until you descend behind houses and cottages to emerge on the edge of Elmslack, near Cove Road.

Turn left and go down to the bottom of Elmslack Lane, where you turn left again by a telephone box, keeping ahead past a Methodist chapel to another road junction. Turn left, and in a short while turn right into Bottoms Lane. Follow Bottoms Lane to a path (signposted) on the left to The Row/Railway Station, and there leave the lane, initially walking beside a wall then heading across fields for the distant hamlet of The Rows. When you get there turn right, up the road (take care again), and go past Bank Well.

Bank Well is an ancient pond formed in the post-glacial period. It was given to the people of Silverdale as a watering place for cattle and horses under enclosure legislation of 1817. The pond, neglected for a long time, was restored between 1994 and 1996.

Tackle one more short rise before descending to a path on the left (signposted Railway Station) that steers the route across Silverdale Golf Course. Keep a wary eye open for low-flying golf balls, and head across the course until the green path descends to a lane near Silverdale Station. Turn right, go past the station and at the first turning on the left, return to Myers Farm (RSPB).

Walk 3: The Four Rivers

Start/Finish: Hornby, car park beside bridge. GR.585683

Distance: 10 miles (16km)

Height gain: Nominal, though there are a few ups and downs

Walking time: 4 hours

Type of Walk: Easy walking, a mix of farmland and riverside wanderings.

Map: OS Landranger Sheet 97: Kendal and Morecambe

Public transport: *Rail:* Wennington, which can be used as an alternative start. *Bus:* MTL, RIB and KIL run to Hornby.

Wenning, Hindburn, Greta and Lune

The Castle Hotel in Hornby, once a coaching inn, testifies to the importance of the village, which stands on a bluff overlooking the Lune Valley, to drovers and other travellers between Lancaster and Kendal. This strategic location and the added height above the low-lying riparian lands, made Hornby a good defensive site, though the impressive Hornby Castle, which incorporates the ruins of an older, possibly thirteenth-century, building, dates only from the sixteenth and nineteenth centuries (1847). The village is a thriving community, divided into two halves by the River Wenning. The oldest of the buildings tend to be to the south of the river, though the imposing castle lies just to the north.

In the days of the Domesday survey (1086) the Lords of Hornby possessed most of the lands of Lonsdale and Craven, and the lordships of Melling and Wennington, the former becoming such a rich parish that it was divided into four 'quarterings'.

More than four centuries later, Edward Stanley of Hornby led Lancashire men into battle at Flodden Field (9 September 1513), when an invading Scottish force led by James IV was heavily defeated by the English, and virtually a whole generation of Scottish nobility wiped out. In return Henry VIII created Stanley, Lord Monteagle, a name linked to the eagle banners that flew over the midmost castle keep. The king heaped honours on Stanley:

Lancashire like lyons layden them about!
All had been lost, by our Lorde.
Had not those leddes bene!

The octagonal tower at the west end of the church was constructed as a Flodden memorial in fulfilment of Stanley's vow that should he return from the field of battle, he would honour his patron saint, St Margaret. Carved upon the tower is Stanley's only memorial: "Lord Monteagle a soldier caused me to be made."

This circular walk can begin just as easily at Wennington, which is visited by a rail service, or indeed at the villages of Wray or Wrayton. Along the way the route is accompanied by four rivers: it travels with the Wenning, the Hindburn and the Greta, before submitting to the greater glory that is the Lune.

Begin from the car park adjoining the southern end of the Wenning bridge in Hornby. Walk back to cross the road, and head along

Hornby Castle

a surfaced track, later fenced, beside the Institute. Keep going to the end of the track, and there pass through a gate and bear left to a gate in a corner. Beyond, cross a stile over a fence on the left and walk across the ensuing field to reach another stile. From here keep half-right over two more stiles and three fields to reach a walled, green lane by a gate. At a track junction go right, through a gate, and cross the former Lancaster to Wennington railway line. This small branch line was one of many that fell to the Beeching axe in 1966, having first operated in the mid-1880s. Once across the trackbed, take a waymarked lane to reach the River Hindburn, and then follow a track between hedges to reach a cross-lane. Turn left and then right, and spend a few unsavoury moments passing the sewage works to reach a bridge over the river. This little loop by-passes the village of Wray, so if you want to go there keep ahead at the cross-lane, and then follow the road through the village to rejoin the route at the bridge.

Wray was once a thriving industrial community making clogs, top hats, nails and baskets, as well as having a silk mill. Its village school was originally endowed by Captain Pooley, a former resident of Wray, who served in Cromwell's army.

Cross the bridge and a white stile on the right. Bear left and then right above a small woodland to head along an old hedge line to reach a road close by a barn. Turn right and walk along the road until opposite the next farm on the right you can cross a stile and stride out across fields. Gates in hedgerows guide you onward to descend to a small footbridge and gate and on up the other side. Press on by stiles and fields, eventually to descend to an old school building and a road. You need to shun the fairly obvious drive running down to the road, and opt instead for a path that crosses a stream and a track to reach a stile in a hedgerow.

Follow the hedge over the next rise, through a small woodland to a stile, and then head downhill and slightly right. This is easier on the ground than might be supposed from a plethora of stile-field-gate-hedgerow instructions that take your mind off the pleasure of easy walking. On the way you can pick out the church at Tatham, dedicated to St James the Less, built in the twelfth century and modified in the fifteenth. Your objective is Overend Farm, from

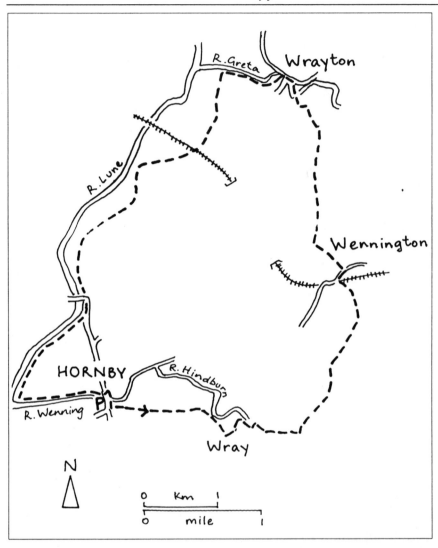

where its access leads down to the road into Wennington. Turn left to reach the railway station, and then right along the road. Another left turn brings you into the village.

Leave the village heading north-west along a back lane to Melling, and passing Wennington Hall on the way. The Hall was first built in 1345, and rebuilt in the mid-1800s by the High Sheriff of Lancaster, William Saunders. Just beyond the second entrance to Wennington Hall, go through a small gate in a wall which is followed by a short stretch in woodland before ascending a small hill ahead. Your next objective is the village of Wrayton, and again the way to it is easier to follow than to describe, being along the line of an old hedgerow interspersed with bits of a wall crossed by stiles. A steep descent finally leads down into Wrayton,

Turn left along the road, leaving it after about 100m/yds to turn right over a stile (signposted). Take to a green track, go through a gate and over a stile, and then follow a wall beside the River Greta, to reach the A683.

Cross the road and rejoin the riverbank. Shortly, follow the embankment on the left, which now swings away from the Greta to parallel the River Lune. The path runs into a walled lane. Turn right on reaching this and keep on to a railway bridge. Beyond, go to the end of the lane and through a gate, following a hedge along the side of a lake.

More stiles lead you on through fields to another embankment near a small stretch of the river known as the Old Lune. Follow the embankment until you reach the main river, and there take to a raised neck of land between trees to reach a gate. Another gate on the right then takes you across a small bridge, around the base of the embankment, and on to reach Loyn Bridge near Castle Stede, probably the best example of a Norman motte and bailey castle in Lancashire, and built at a very strategic crossing point of the river. It was erected in something of a hurry in the unsettled and dangerous days of King Stephen (1135-54), a wooden keep on a heaped mound surrounded by a ditch and wooden stockade.

From this point you can hasten back to Hornby along the road (a stile near the ramparts of Castle Stede gives access to the road), and save about a mile of legwork. Otherwise press on beneath Loyn Bridge, built in 1684 to replace a ford at this point, and through an untidy woodland then to follow the Lune to its confluence with the Wenning. Turn left here and follow the Wenning back to Hornby. The path rises on to floodbanks and turns to meet the road at the northern end of the Wenning bridge.

Walk 4: Green Hill

Start/Finish: Near Leck Fell House. GR.674791. There is ample room on the left of the road to park cars without causing obstruction.

Distance: 7¼ miles (12km)

Height gain: 1180ft (360m)

Walking time: 3½-4 hours

Type of Walk: Almost entirely on grass, with very little bog. The return journey involves descending a wild, tussocky and untracked fellside until a farm track is reached.

Map: OS Outdoor Leisure Map 1:25 000: Sheet 2: Yorkshire Dales Western area.

Public transport: MTL and RIB operate limited services through Cowan Bridge.

The Summit of Lancashire

There is a Green Hill far away beside a lonely wall. It lies in the top right hand corner of Lancashire, amid a wild stretch of moorland, and at 628 metres (2060 feet) is now the highest summit in the county. A few paces to the right (assuming you could take them without the obstruction of a substantial drystone wall) and you would be in Cumbria; one metre less in height and it would share the distinction of being Lancashire's highest with its adjoining fell, Gragareth, which for a while, until resurveying proved otherwise, was thought of as the most elevated point. Green Hill forms part of a rising grassy ridge that starts with Gragareth, and culminates at its northernmost end with a higher summit, Great Coum, in Cumbria and overlooking Dentdale.

The easiest approach is from Leck, which permits a pleasing circuit equally suitable for occasional walkers and the more regular frequenters of our hills. Leck is a small and quiet village lying just off the A65, a short distance south-east of Kirkby Lonsdale, and close by Cowan Bridge where the Brontë sisters attended a school for clergymen's daughters. Cowan Bridge and Ireby, a short way further south, both afford access to Leck, and from there to a metalled roadway running into the great hollow of the hills as far as Leck Fell House, surely the most isolated inhabited dwelling in Lancashire.

There are two ample parking areas near Leck Fell House still an active farm and you should begin from there. But please note: there are no rights of way or legitimate access routes on to these fine hills, but well-behaved walkers have enjoyed unrestricted use for years. Be considerate.

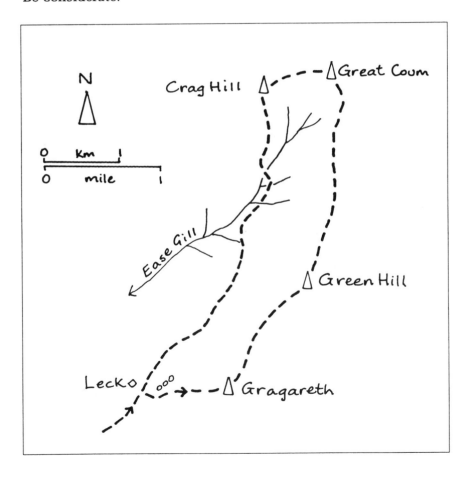

Begin along the road to a gate on the right, just before Leck Fell House, beyond which a broad track heads out across the lower slopes of Gragareth. You can follow this track for a short distance if you wish, or take immediately to the hillside. Either way your immediate objective is the stand of three stone pillars, the Three Men of Gragareth, prominent from your starting point, but not from the track below them. They were probably built by the men who constructed the drystone walls that network these fells.

From the Three Men head east over easily sloping ground until you either hit the trig point marking the highest point, or the wall beyond, which marks the county boundary. On a clear day the view is superb! Barbondale and the Howgills lie close by, while to the west the winding River Lune and the spreading mud flats of Morecambe Bay slip out to the distant horizon.

To continue to Green Hill and Great Coum, simply follow the wall, a remarkably well-constructed affair that might have been meant to keep Lancastrians and Yorkshiremen apart in days gone by. You stroll easily over Green Hill, all the way to Great Coum, having to negotiate only one wall, and that by a convenient gate. Just beyond the gate, where its wall and the ridge wall meet, you find the County Stone, a large, primeval boulder where the old counties of Lancashire, Westmorland and West Riding met.

Further on, up a slight rise, the top of Great Coum is adorned by an impressive and large cairn. It stands on the north side of the ridge wall, and there is no easy way to it. The cairn does not mark the highest point of the hill, though it is regarded as such. The true summit is a vague spot height, 687 metres (GR.701836), impossible to reach without climbing walls, and neither worth the trouble nor encouraged.

To return to Leck Fell House, continue along the wall to Crag Hill, and from there descend untracked ground to the confluence of Long Gill and Ease Gill. Ascend gradually from the becks, aiming for the intake wall above Ease Gill where you will pick up a narrow path leading in due course to the broad track on which you started this round. The rest of the journey is a simple and relaxing stroll, for the most part steadily easing downwards.

Walk 5: Upper Lonsdale

Start/Finish: Car park adjoining Leck church. GR.643767

Distance: 6 miles (10km)

Height gain: Nominal

Walking time: 2½-3½ hours

Type of Walk: Easy walking through rolling pastureland.

Map: OS Landranger 97: Kendal and Morecambe

Public transport: *Bus:* HEY and RIB run services to Cowan Bridge.

Leck Loop

This circular tour of the countryside between the villages of Leck and Tunstall begins from a small car park at St Peter's Church in Leck. The church was built in 1878-9 by Paley and Austin, though it was badly damaged by fire in 1912 (some sources say 21 October 1913). In 1915, it was rededicated having been quickly rebuilt, closely copying the original.

From the church go right, to a T-junction, and then slightly left to a stone stile. Through the stile cross the ensuing field to reach a lane, and beyond that another stile that gives you access to Leck Beck. Turn left following the beck side, under an old railway bridge and then up to the road at Cowan Bridge.

Here at Cowan Bridge is the plain house that Carus Wilson, vicar of Tunstall, founded in 1823 (1824?) the school for clergymen's daughters that was attended by the Brontë sisters. The original school was immortalised in a biography of Charlotte and as Lowood in *Jane Eyre*, and now forms part of a row of terraced cottages; the school was transferred to nearby Casterton in 1833. Wilson was quite an enterprising man and edited two penny papers, the first of their kind in England, the *Friendly Visitor* and *Children's Friend*.

Cross the road, turn right and cross the bridge and then go down to a path on the left leading down to the beck once more. Follow this as far as the footbridge giving access back across the beck to the hamlet of Overtown. Along the way you cross the line of a Roman road, which here runs almost exactly north-south; you will cross it again later in the walk.

As you come into Overtown, turn right and follow the road for

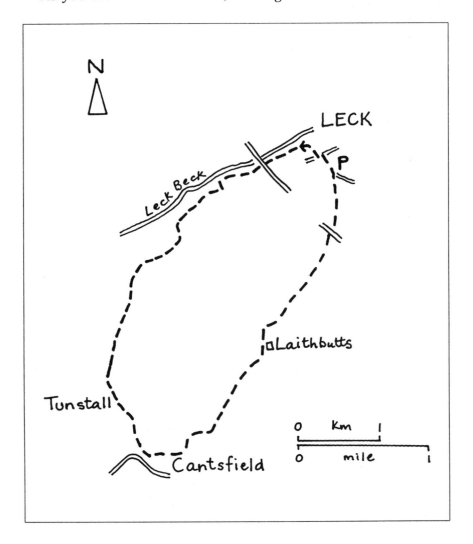

almost a mile (1.5km) until, at a sharp right bend, you leave it, continuing roughly in a southerly direction along a track to reach Churchfield House Farm. The path passes between the farmhouse and a barn to continue down the farm drive to a lane.

Just off to the right here is Tunstall church, dedicated to St John the Baptist, and described by Nikolaus Pevsner as, "The only church in North Lancashire which one can praise for never having given in to sweeping suggestions to restore windows and other features. It creates a human appeal which cannot otherwise be roused." The church, said to be Charlotte Brontë's Bricklebridge Church (*Jane Eyre*), dates from the thirteenth century, but was rebuilt around 1415 by Sir Thomas Tunstall. Jessica Lofthouse describes how the pupils at the school in Cowan Bridge used to walk to Tunstall church on Sunday mornings to attend matins, then ate a packed lunch in a room above the church doorway and awaited evensong.

Away to your right stands Thurland Castle, moated residence of Sir Brian Tunstall, and once described as an "ancient" castle, but as you see it now better ascribed as the handiwork of the same architects, Paley and Austin, who built Leck church.

Cross the lane and keep ahead. Cross a field to a bridge and gate, followed by another field. Target a gate in the left corner, and there turn right along a hedgerow. The route now becomes a well-defined track, and when this bends left, keep forward to a gate. Go through this then left twice, the second time at a farm on the edge of Cantsfield, keeping a stream on your left. Go over a bridge and along a fenced lane leading shortly into woodland.

This lane leads in a roughly north-easterly direction, recrossing the line of the Roman road to reach Laithbutts, where it goes north for a short distance before resuming its north-easterly direction. As you go the track improves and eventually passes beneath the old railway line encountered earlier near Cowan Bridge. Go under this, cross the A65 and up steps opposite to a gap stile. Follow a wall adjoining a private garden and then cross the ensuing field until the wall ends and is replaced by a hedgerow.

After two stiles, cross a footbridge and go through two gates to reach a road just south of Leck church and your starting point.

Walk 6: Lancaster to Glasson Dock

Start/Finish: Lancaster city centre bus station. GR.477619

Distance: 12 miles (19km)

Height gain: None

Walking time: 4-5 hours

Type of Walk: Easy walking along railway trackbed and canal towpath.

Map: OS Pathfinder 648: Lancaster and Morecambe, and 659: Galgate and Dolphinholme.

Public transport: Bus and rail services operate into Lancaster, and AOR run a bus service between Lancaster and Glasson Dock.

Ancient Ways

Both the River Lune and the Lancaster Canal are ancient routes by which commerce plied the seaports of the western coast and further afield. Glasson Dock, where this walk turns round and returns, was developed when silting of the river estuary prevented sea-going vessels from reaching Lancaster.

This walk can be started either from Glasson Dock or, as described here, in the city centre. There are numerous car parks in Lancaster, but with the possibility of a start from the mainline railway, and an excellent bus service to and from Lancaster operated by National Express, there is much to commend the use of public transport to reach the city.

From the bus station in Lancaster take the road that leads out below the castle, under the old and new railway lines and along St George's Quay. All this early walking is on a paved surface, but this ends after about a mile (1.5km), near an industrial estate. From here keep on down a track (a bridleway known as Mile Lane), and beyond a cross-track known as Freeman's Wood. Mile Lane ends at a field gate, and there you turn left and instantly right on to the Lancashire

Lancaster Canal, Galgate

Coastal Way, which here commandeers the old railway line from Glasson Dock to Lancaster. As a result the route description is the easiest possible, with the possible exception of the return leg along the canal, about which more anon.

Follow the old trackbed, which saw service from 1883 until 1964, until it reaches Conder Green, where a diversion to the Stork Inn for refreshments may be in order, though there are more opportunities in Glasson Dock and along the Glasson Branch of the canal at the Millers Pub, Thurnham. On the way the scope for birdwatching is second-to-none, and the mudflats provide food and shelter for a wide range of coastal birds, making a pair of binoculars essential on this walk.

As you approach Conder Green, the route goes through a picnic site, built in an old cutting. The continuing track to Glasson Dock bears right immediately after leaving the picnic site, and finally reaches Glasson beside the road and the Victoria Inn.

The village of Glasson was originally a farming settlement until

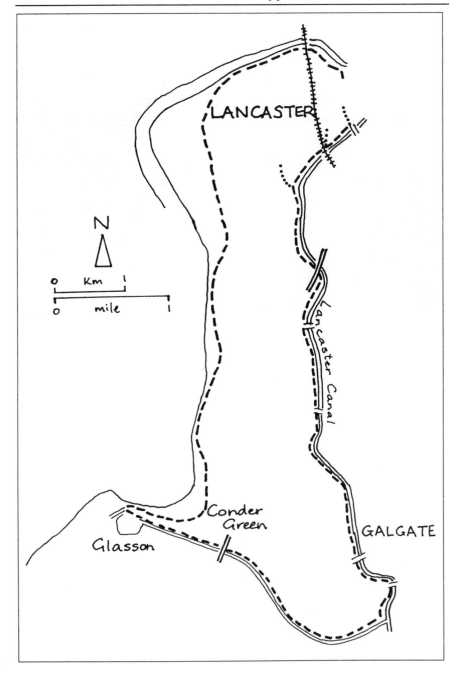

the dock was built in 1787. It was intended to accommodate up to 25 sea-going ships, but now hosts a deluge of leisure craft. The canal was built in 1825, and links with the main Lancaster Canal.

Having explored Glasson, cross the car park opposite the Victoria, and following the towpath, go left. This runs on for 2½ miles (4km) until it meets the main canal, where all you need to do is turn left and follow the towpath back to Lancaster. As you come into Lancaster you can leave the canal at any one of a number of points for a return through the streets of this historic town.

The canal was built between 1797 and 1819, and stretches almost 60 miles (100km) from Preston through Lancaster to Kendal, and offers a diversity of wildlife that is virtually unrivalled in the county. It is still navigable between Preston and Tewitfield, north of Lancaster, a fact well known to canal boating enthusiasts.

Walk 7: The Lune Valley

Start: Green Ayre Park on Parliament Street, Lancaster. GR.479622

Finish: Devil's Bridge, Kirkby Lonsdale.

Distance: 16½ miles (26km)

Height gain: Virtually none

Walking time: 5-6 hours

Type of Walk: Easy, waymarked walk, never far from the River Lune. The going underfoot is likely to be wet and muddy, so boots or wellies are needed.

Maps: OS Pathfinder 648: Lancaster and Morecambe; and 637: Burton-in-Kendal and Caton; OS Landranger 97: Kendal and Morecambe.

Public transport: *Rail:* West coast and local service to Lancaster (no service to Kirkby Lonsdale). *Bus:* KIL operates between Kirkby Lonsdale and Lancaster.

In a Luneside World

Recommended by Wordsworth in his *Guide to the Lakes* as the only way to approach Kendal from the south, and painted by the artist Turner, it is not surprising that the Vale of Lune, east of Lancaster in particular, is popular with visitors. Part of this outstanding walk beside the River Lune follows the trackbed of the Lancaster-Wennington railway along which gradients are virtually non-existent. The route is also a cycleway, so expect wheeled-wonders to go whirling by from time to time.

The walk links the city of Lancaster with the market town of Kirkby Lonsdale, two historic centres. On the way it passes by or through attractive villages, castles and ancient churches, and never moves far from the delectable River Lune, a charming companion, if you don't already have one. Perversely, I enjoy this walk in poor weather, even when it is raining, snugly clad in warm and weather-

Sunset, Glasson Dock

proof clothing, enveloped in my own little Luneside world. At any stage of the walk you can simply turn round and walk back, or keep going to the end and catch the bus back from Kirkby Lonsdale.

The opportunity to explore Lancaster, either before or after this walk, should not be disregarded; it is a truly fascinating city, one that is proud of its heritage and doesn't mind letting you know. If you don't know Lancaster, contact the tourism office for information (01524 32878).

Start from Green Ayre Park on Parliament Street (A6) in Lancaster and set off past Skerton Bridge. Skerton Bridge holds an important place in Lancaster's history. The original bridge spanning the Lune at this point was made of wood, and probably existed before the thirteenth century. The first mention of it, however, dates from 1215, when King John instructed that the Abbey at Furness should be granted timber from the Forest of Lancaster to repair the bridge. By 1590 the condition of the bridge, damaged by the passage of heavy goods, was bad and the cause of great concern. As Border

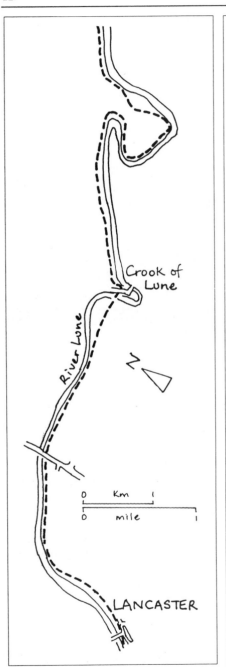

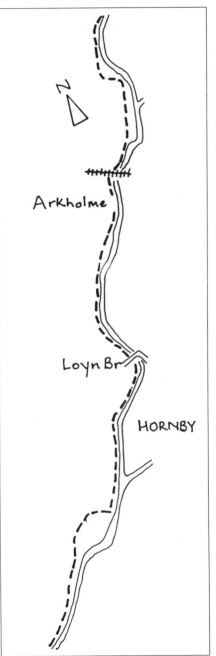

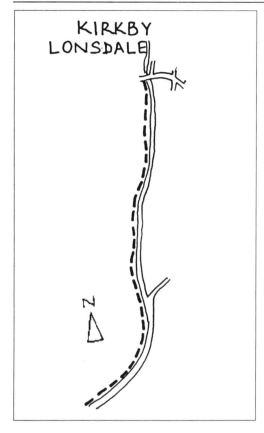

reivers approached the town in 1715, the suggestion was put forward that the bridge should be demolished to safeguard the town, but this did not happen because it was pointed out that the river could be forded quite easily anyway. By 1770, the town authorities were looking at the possibility of building a new bridge, but the present bridge was not completed until 1787, the first bridge in England to have a flat carriageway across it, instead of the more conventional humpbacked arrangement.

Skerton Weir, a short distance further on, was built more than 300 years ago to reduce the risk of tidal salt water flowing upstream. Beyond the weir you go under the aqueduct carrying the Lancaster-Kendal canal over the Lune. Keeping with the Lune, you shortly pass beneath the M6 motorway, and after another half mile reach Denny Beck car park. Keep going, maintaining faith with the Lune.

At the Crook of Lune, picnic tables beside the river waylay the well-intentioned, especially in spring and summer. At other times of year you can have the whole beautiful landscape to yourself, a few sheep, and the mallards, moorhens and goosanders that patrol the river and its meadows. Here the track keeps ahead to cross the looping river twice, and then starts heading away from it on the approach to Caton. Unless you want a short walk, you now leave the old trackbed. The line was known as the 'Little' North Western, to distinguish it from its greater counterpart. It survived for about a hundred years before succumbing to the Beeching Axe in 1966.

As you reach the railway bridge at Crook o'Lune, don't cross it, but go left, either down steps or a serpentine ramp to reach a gate giving into a riverside meadow. Follow the river's edge, but not too closely, the banks are being undermined in a few places. A gate and stile lead you into another field that comes to an end down by the water's edge, where a stile leads you into woodland.

The path through the woodland undulates, and is an excellent place from which to watch the birds on the river and among the trees. The woodland comes to an end quite abruptly at a stile crossing a barbed wire fence. Cross the stile and go left, gradually moving away from the fenceline to aim for a footbridge spanning an in-flowing stream. Beyond that looms the massive ironwork structure of a bridge carrying the Thirlmere Aqueduct, and tempting as it might be to cross the river at this point, returning down the other side, access to the bridge is prohibited.

Keeping towards the river, a path leads you to a stile at the entrance to yet another wooded copse, Lawson's Wood, in which you immediately cross a footbridge before strolling on through the mixed woodland.

Further on, just south-west of Aughton (pronounced Afton), the path descends to a prominent bend in the river, a meander that needs to be faithfully followed before resuming a north-easterly course. A few minutes onward the route performs a dog-leg and then presses on past, on the far side of the river, the confluence with the Wenning, the main tributary of the Lune, and rising not far away among the fells of the Forest of Bowland. Before long the path reaches three-arched Loyn Bridge, a construction that dates from medieval times, and the only road crossing of the river between the Crook o'Lune and Kirkby Lonsdale. Nearby, overlooking the eastern end of the bridge, is the mound of Norman earthwork known as Castle Stede.

An interesting stone through-stile gives on to the road beside Loyn Bridge, from where, for a short while, the river now heads north-wards before bearing north-eastwards again towards the village of

Arkholme, an ancient Norse settlement, with cottages dating from the seventeenth century. Near Newton the route uses a short stretch of permissive footpath granted by the Newton Hall Estate, beyond which the walk courts the riverbank almost faithfully all the remaining way to Kirkby Lonsdale.

The end of the walk is marked by Devil's Bridge, another of medieval construction, on the edge of Kirkby Lonsdale, and just in Cumbria. The town developed largely on the strength of passing packhorse trade in centuries gone by, and during the eighteenth century was noted all around for its annual hiring fairs.

John Ruskin much admired Kirkby Lonsdale, declaring that here was moorland, sweet river, and English forest at their best. Stone age burial mounds lie on the surrounding hills, and the strategic importance of the site was not missed by the Romans, who built a camp close by.

In one of the recesses of Devil's Bridge is a small stone column which some opinions consider could be a plague stone. These were often to be found at the edge of towns stricken by plague, so that well-wishers might place offerings of food.

Walk 8: Cockersand Abbey

Start/Finish: Glasson Dock car park. GR.448560

Distance: 8¾ miles (14km)

Height gain: None

Walking time: 3½-4 hours

Type of Walk: Easy coastal and pastureland walking.

Map: Pathfinder 659: Galgate and Dolphinholme

Public transport: *Bus:* AOR to Lancaster – Glasson Dock.

By Abbey and Mossy Lanes

Although its heyday has long since gone, Glasson Dock still sees service as a marina and safe haven for leisure craft. Formerly, it was developed to accommodate sea-going vessels that, because of silting up of the River Lune, could no longer reach to the heart of Lancaster. Its construction was financed by the businessmen of Lancaster, and permitted under the provisions of two separate Acts of Parliament in 1738 and 1749. In 1826 the Lancaster Canal was extended to Glasson, allowing goods to travel the canal network between Kendal, Lancaster, Preston and further south.

This pleasant circular begins at Glasson Dock and runs out to overlook the Lune Estuary and Cockerham Sands before turning inland to visit the village of Thurnham and returning along a short stretch of the Glasson branch of the canal.

Start from the car park (small charge) adjoining the B5290 and the Glasson Basin, and turn left to cross the basin swing bridge. Keep on up Tithebarn Hill, past the post office, and at the top bear left with the road for a first glimpse across the Glasson Marsh which, like much of this coastline, is host to thousands of wading and sea birds.

Follow the road a short way further until at a sharp left bend you

Cockersand Abbey

can leave it, turning right into Marsh Lane (bridleway sign), and going down past a caravan site to reach open pastureland at a gate. A short stretch of 'muddy' walking ensues as the track enters an open field often grazed by cows. Keep ahead beside a line of old hawthorns and bear left with the track as it moves away from the hawthorns to a gate, beyond which the track runs up to Crook Farm on the coast.

On reaching the farm, go left along the Lancashire Coastal Way, following a surfaced drive, and stay with this coast-hugging track, past the end of Slack Lane and its nearby car park, to reach Cockersand Abbey.

Cockersand Abbey began as a hermitage in about 1180, and became an abbey of the Premonstratensian Order ten years later. In 1539 the abbot and 22 canons surrendered it to the King's Commissioners, and it has lain in ruins ever since. This site was the hermitage of Hugh Garth, whose reputation led to the establishment on this site of a hospital for lepers, and ten years later the priory. In time the priory became wealthy enough to acquire the rank of abbey, and owned property throughout much of Lancashire and the Lake District.

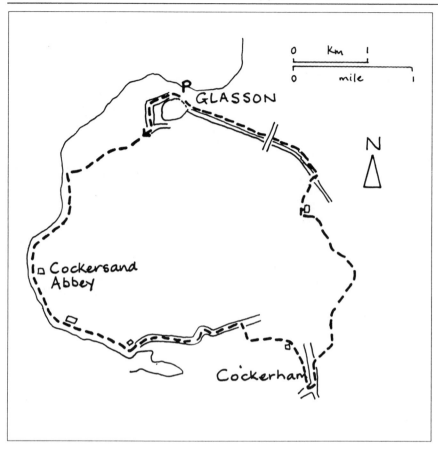

A brief diversion is necessary to inspect the abbey ruins, but having done so a short stroll across coastal turf takes you back to the edge of the estuary. Follow this now to Bank Houses. As you approach Bank Houses, leave the grassy path and drop below a wall on to a concrete walkway that leads you out past ruined buildings to a surfaced lane at a gate. Keep ahead (east), keeping the caravan park on your left, following a narrow path, and in time you reach another caravan site at Bank End Farm.

Press on past Bank End Farm, beyond which a surfaced lane runs east. An adjoining embankment (not a right of way) provides a more elevated view of coastal pastures that often provide a wealth of ornithological interest. Stay with the lane to reach the village of

Hillam. Keep on through the village to a footpath about 300m/yds beyond the village on the right. Turn right, through a gate, on to a broad cart track, and when the track shortly bends left, go ahead through another gate, following a field boundary with a drainage ditch and fence on the left. This guides you to a footbridge over a stream, beyond which you aim more or less ahead towards Ware Cottage, preceded by a low step stile. Cross in front of the cottage, beyond which an access lane runs out to the A588. As the access bends left, keep ahead over two stiles, and then bear half left to another stile in a top field corner giving into a builder's compound. Press on, between buildings, to reach a lane descending into the village of Cockerham.

On reaching the road in Cockerham, go left with it along the A588 as far as the access, on the right, to Batty Hill Farm. Keep ahead through the farm buildings, then curving left to descend a sunken trackway flanked by sycamore trees. Keep on through a gate and on ahead along a muddy cart track. This brings you to a series of gates along a hedged lane until you reach a waymark sending you left into a wide pasture. Head across the pasture, towards Cock Hall Farm. Keep a pond to your right, and cross a footbridge, then head for the buildings of Cock Hall Farm ahead.

Waymarks guide you through the farm buildings, and out on to its access lane, which takes you unerringly to the village of Thurnham. Go past the church (1785) and follow the track round through mixed woodland until you can turn right in front of Thurnham Hall Country Club. Go past the hall, down a broad track, and after a group of derelict farm buildings, bear right. A short way on, look for a waymark on an ash tree on the left, near an old gateway. Go left here through the obsolete gateway, and then ahead across a pasture into a scruffy lane with hedges that is often wet and muddy. When you reach a ladder stile, go over the stile and bear right to reach Bailey Bridge on the branch canal. Cross the bridge, but do not go through the gate on the other side. Instead, squeeze through a narrow stile on the left and descend rough steps to the canal towpath.

The canal towpath now steers you pleasantly back to Glasson Dock, passing The Millers pub, formerly Thurnham Mill, on the right. Take care as you cross the Conder Green road (A588) before rejoining the towpath for the final stage back to Glasson.

Walk 9: Littledale

Start/Finish: Roadside parking near Little Cragg Farm. GR.546617

Distance: 5 miles (8km)

Height gain: 330ft (100m)

Walking time: 2-2½ hours

Type of Walk: Easy walking, with some undulation, mostly on good paths or farm tracks.

Map: OS Pathfinder 637: Burton-in-Kendal & Caton

Public transport: HEY, RIB and KIL operate services along the A683 calling at Caton, 2miles/3km from the nearest point of this walk.

They Don't Make Diamonds as Big as Bricks

The tiny enclave of Littledale conceals itself shyly among the folds of the hills south of Caton, an unsuspected gem that provides the opportunity for a little peaceful wandering through wooded cloughs and glens, across slopes of bracken and soft green, flower-decked turf.

The walk begins from a car park (on both sides of the road) at Little Cragg at the highest point of the Littledale Road. It is best reached from Caton, from where Littledale is signposted, between the Station Hotel and a garage. After about a mile (1.6km) keep with the Littledale sign, and soon go right to Brookhouse. You are now on Littledale Road and this takes you to a junction at New House Farm where you turn right (signposted Quernmore) and drive steeply uphill to the roadside parking spaces.

From here, begin by walking back down the road and across Artle Beck and on towards New House Farm. Turn right and go through Crossgill to a sharp bend about 250m/yds further on, where you leave the road for a cart track (grass) that takes you into woodland. As you leave the woodland you encounter a former church, built in

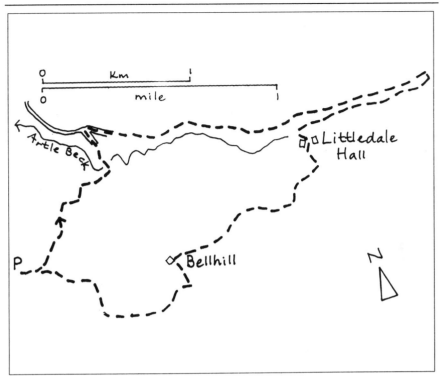

1849 by the Vicar of Cockerham, John Dodson, who also built the collection of buildings at Littledale Hall.

As you reach the end of a wall, the track forks. Go left and in about half a mile (1km) stay below a fence when the track goes into a field. Keep on through the top end of a wood and emerge to cross a stream and climb steeply for a few strides. Now the path goes along a broad green track above the river for another half a mile (1km), with good views of the deeply cut and well-wooded profile of Littledale ahead.

When the path expires you drop to a ford and a ruined bridge. Set off back along a lower track beside a stream, the product of many side streams that feed in from the surrounding fells. The path enters woodland just above Littledale Hall. Soon, cross a bridge leading to the Hall, turn left and go through a complex of chicken-rearing buildings to turn right through a gate at their end.

A track takes you into woodland again and over Foxdale Beck by a bridge, soon after which the track bends sharply right, and zigzags up through woodland to emerge into a field. Keep ahead to a wall corner where a stone step stile takes you on to Field Head Farm, a remote steading. Go across to the farm access and follow it to Bell Hill Farm, with, on a fine day, a view out across Morecambe Bay.

At Bell Hill Farm go through a gate and left in the yard, following a track down to a ford and footbridge over Uldale Beck. Beyond, go up a field into woodland again on a track that takes you to Skelbow Barn. At the barn go through a gate on the right on to a grassy track that goes down a field, through another gate, past a barn and up to the road. Your starting point is up to your left.

Walk 10: Garstang and the Lancaster Canal

Start/Finish: Riverside car park, Garstang. GR.492449

Distance: 7 miles (11km)

Height gain: Nominal

Walking time: 3-4 hours

Type of Walk: Easy walking across fields and farm tracks, finishing along a canal towpath.

Map: OS Pathfinder Sheet 668: Garstang

Public transport: *Bus:* RIB, BPT and HRY all operate services to Garstang.

Kirkland and Nateby Wander

This delightful walk tours the countryside around Garstang before returning down an agreeable stretch of the Lancaster Canal. It is a fine walk to contemplate as the autumn days draw close in, when a flask of something hot and a bite to eat would be welcome companions. Remember to wear or carry something warm.

For hundreds of years, certainly from the beginning of the fourteenth century, Garstang was a natural meeting place and an important trading centre for the Fylde coast, and its prosperity flourished because of the constant passage of travellers and the yarn, linen and cotton industries that developed in the neighbourhood. The town was granted a charter by Charles II, and it became the chief market for corn, fish and cattle. The Romans constructed a crossing of the River Wyre at this point, and their route was followed by the eighteenth-century turnpike.

In 1864 the construction of a railway across the Fylde mosses was authorised under the provisions of the Garstang and Knott End

Railway Act, but it was not until 1908 that the railway was finally extended to Knott End, a quiet community set across the Wyre estuary from Fleetwood, which has steadfastly refused to pursue the touristic trends of its neighbouring coastal partners. Sadly, the railway line was not economical, and it effectively committed suicide long before the Beeching axe fell.

The walk begins from the riverside car park in Garstang and from it you go right, along the riverside path, to join the road near Wyre Bridge. Go across the bridge, then right, beneath the arch of the Garstang Corn Mill. Keep beside the old mill race and the River Wyre to pass below the aqueduct that conveys the Lancaster Canal over the river, an ingenious piece of handiwork, designed in 1793 by the same man who designed London Bridge and Waterloo Bridge.

Go up steps on the far side to gain the towpath and turn left. After a short while you come to a stile just before the canal basin. Cross the stile and the playing field beyond, heading half left on a path known as Many Pads, to a gate in a fence. Then keep straight ahead across two fields to touch upon the riverbank once more and to follow it into the next field, there keeping ahead to reach the A6.

Cross this busy road and go left past Cross House Farm to a track signposted to Kirkland Hall. Go right along this track, past a farm and Hagg Wood to enter a field. Turn left, and leave through a gate in a corner, then keeping ahead towards Kirkland Hall (originally constructed in 1760, though some of the building was carried out during the seventeenth century). Join an enclosed track at a gate on the right. Keep along the track to a junction, and there turn right to Hall Farm, and left along a cobbled road past the farm itself.

When the road bends left, go ahead through a gate and turn right down another track (north-west), soon to leave one field and enter another. The track ends at a bridge over a small stream, Ains Pool. Keep ahead (barn on the far left), and head for a stile in a fence. Cross the stile and stick close to the ensuing fence for a short distance, to reach and cross a slab bridge and a stile at the top of the field.

Once more keep close to the field margin on your right, and when you meet a fence, go left to a stile near a gate in the field's left corner. Keep on past a pond and along the left side of a field to Humblescough Lane. Go right to Longmoor Lane in the hamlet of Nateby.

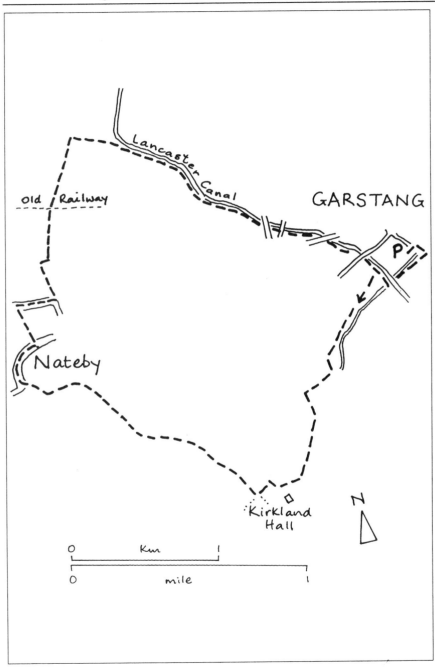

Leave Nateby past a school and the post office, and leave Long-moor Lane after the last house, turning left at a metal gate to walk along an enclosed lane to the corner of a triangular field, leaving it at a corner gate into Kilcrash Lane, near Hool House. Turn right along Kilcrash Lane and soon look for a signposted path to Winmar-leigh Hall, though you are not going so far.

Go over a footbridge and through Bowers Wood, then along a field track, turning left at a corner before a gateway. Keep on until you reach a disused railway trackbed, the old Knott End railway line. Cross the trackbed, go over a stile and into a field, keeping close to the hedge on your left. Ignore a stile luring you into a copse, but keep resolutely on to a facing hedgerow to join the farm access to Nateby Hall.

Go right, to reach the Lancaster Canal and the certainty that all the difficult navigation is over. Follow the canal towpath back to Garstang as far as the aqueduct. From the aqueduct retrace your steps to the start.

Walk 11: Langden Round

Start/Finish: Langden Brook, near Sykes. GR.632512. Off-road parking near access road.

Distance: 5½ miles (9km)

Height gain: 1490 feet (455m)

Walking time: 3½-4 hours

Type of Walk: Not advised in poor visibility; a high moorland walk of moderate standard, but with little shelter.

Map: OS Outdoor Leisure Map 41: Forest of Bowland and Ribblesdale

Public transport: Bowland Rambler (40) and Bowland Pathfinder (44) May to September.

For the Love of Wild Places

The Trough of Bowland has been a notorious, as well as a commonplace, thoroughfare for centuries. Through it the so-called Pendle witches were transported for trial at Lancaster Castle in 1612, and it was used as an access route for Scots reivers on their hit-and-run cattle rustling raids that were a feature of the 300-hundred-year war of attrition known as the Border Troubles. The Civil War (1642-9), too, brought its share of attention to this lonely spot; while less angst-ridden crossings were made by everyday wayfarers searching for food and lodging, and by the legitimate work-people of this ancient Forest of Bowland.

To the south Fair Snape Fell is a high and rewarding outing for any lover of wild moorlands, a fine objective that leads you through pleasant dales on to high, heathery hill tops, where the air is keen and the breeze a constant companion. Much of the land travelled by this walk forms a water catchment area, but the introduction of a loop of permissive paths in the mid-1990s brought into legitimacy a walk that many had been doing for years.

Along Langden Beck, Bowland

You start not far from Sykes Farm, setting off along a straight access road that leads to the former Preston Water Works, beyond which you enter the open dale fashioned by Langden Brook, a scene which features on the cover of the first (1996) edition of the excellent and much-needed Ordnance Survey Outdoor Leisure map for this area. A good track heads up-dale to reach the impressive-sounding Langden Castle, but there are no moats, draw-bridges or towering battlements here, just a simple barn with a pretentious name.

Beyond Langden Castle, a signposted path sets off over the billowing fells to Bleasdale. Follow this, and soon you are faced with the prospect of gaining the opposite bank of Langden Brook, a wide stream that has escorted you so far. After prolonged rain the brook, though now much less wide, can be awkward to cross, so do take care, and if you are not happy about your ability to do so safely, turn back, you can always return another day. Normally, however, there is no problem getting over to reach the conspicuous ascending path you will see ahead.

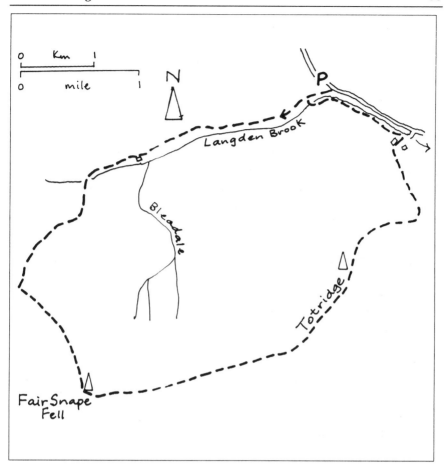

The on-going path is a fine romp, a little steep for a while, but then beginning an exhilarating traverse above the unsuspected and steep-sided ravine of Fiensdale to emerge amid a landscape of shallow peat groughs, bedrock and (especially in autumn) fragrant heather. This is an invigorating place; no dramatic, sculpted scenes, but a wide, open expanse of heather and tussock grass, and walking country as good as any in the Pennines.

The path you have been travelling has thus far been a right of way, but on reaching a fence you must leave it in order to reach Fair Snape Fell. If you keep to the left of the fence, which used to mark the boundary between Lancashire and Yorkshire, you remain on land in the ownership of North West Water who have agreed a concessionary path up to the summit, marked by a large cairn. To the south of the fence you are on Access Land, and free to roam, but the path on that side holds no great advantage, though it can offer slightly easier going when, later on, a few peat groughs are encountered.

The highest point of Fair Snape Fell lies near a fence junction and is marked by a large cairn with a pole projecting from it (for the time being at least). To the south-west a trig pillar, shelter and proliferation of small cairns marks the culmination of the walk for those who have ascended via Parlick (see Walk 18), and this is often regarded as the summit of the fell. It is certainly more imposing, but purists will shun it.

On past the summit, keeping the fence on your right, you continue along the concessionary path, eastwards. A minor deviation to pass around the head of Hareden Brook then leads onward to the trig on Totridge, a neat ridge with a fine view, before continuing in a north-easterly direction and descending steeply to meet a bridleway that will guide you, left (north-west-ish) to Hareden Farm. Take the farm access out towards the valley road, but before crossing Langden Brook, go left on another concessionary path that parallels the brook back to a footbridge near your starting point. Over the footbridge turn right to return to the road, often, on summer weekends, thronged by visitors and mobile refreshments vans.

Note: Dogs are not permitted on the concessionary routes at any time. Walkers may be restricted from access for operational and conservation reasons, on shooting days (between August and December), and at times of high fire risk.

Walk 12: Ward's Stone

Start/Finish: Lee Bridge. GR.567552. You could just as easily start at the Jubilee Tower (GR.542573), where there is better parking.

Distance: 18½ km (11½ miles)

Height gain: 1540ft (470 metres)

Walking time: 5 hours

Type of Walk: Most of this energetic walk is along agreed access routes, from which you cannot deviate. As a result, route-finding, other than in the poorest visibility, is not a problem, and the route seldom in doubt.

Map: OS Outdoor Leisure Map 41: Forest of Bowland and Ribblesdale

Public transport: Bowland Rambler (40) and Bowland Pathfinder (44) May to September.

More than a Stone's Throw

Lying well to the side of the main thrust of the Pennines, the secretive, folded hills of Bowland, have, paradoxically, long been a place of popular resort for the discerning folk of Lancashire. Much of the land of Bowland has known restricted access for many years, with few real opportunities for walkers to stretch their legs. But this fine traverse of Ward's Stone, the highest of the Bowland summits, is available, even though in one sense it serves only to emphasise what you are missing.

You start from Lee Bridge, from whence a surfaced lane follows the Tarnbrook Wyre to the hamlet of Tarnbrook at the confluence of Tarnsyke Clough, Thrush and Gables Cloughs. This tiny, sequestered hamlet was once the centre of a small industry manufacturing gloves and felt hats. Here the roadway gives way to a broad farm access track that soon runs along the course of Higher Syke. Follow this as it continues as a permissive path, ascending the flank of Tarnbrook Fell high above the upper Tarnbrook Wyre. For a while

Ward Stone, highest summit in Bowland, with Ingleborough beyond

the path escapes the clutches of the infant river, but rejoins it as the two bully their way through a narrow ravine, blessed with a fine display of cascades.

Above the falls, you cross the stream and follow a line of posts, ascending north-east to the col between Wolfhole Crag and Ward's Stone, near a small puddle known as Brown Syke. At the col, a fenceline and drystone wall meet, and here you turn left, following the wall to a stile over a fence. Cross this, and continue following the fence uphill, channelled to a point at which fences meet, where you can cross the fence once more, by a stile.

Not far away, stands a trig pillar, one of two on Ward's Stone. By just one metre, the first trig you encounter is higher than the second, though it doesn't look it. The summit plateau is largely bare, dotted with outcrops of gritstone boulders and littered with rocks. From the top, there is a fine panorama, north and east especially, to the Three Peaks of Yorkshire, and north-west to the purple-blue uplands of the Lakeland fells.

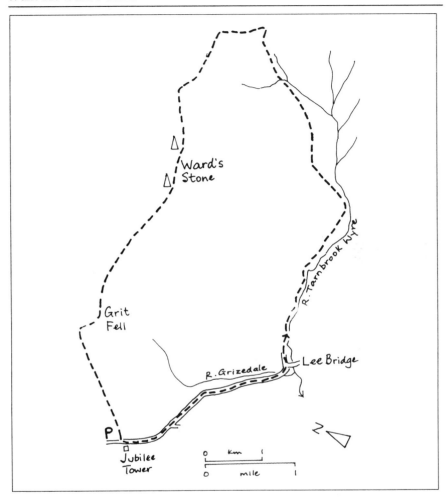

So far you have been following an agreed access strip, and this continues west past the second trig, and onwards to a minor summit, Grit Fell. Just beyond, the route changes direction, heading southwest, and dropping in a straight line to the Jubilee Tower, erected in 1887 by James Harrison of nearby Hare Appletree Farm in commemoration of Queen Victoria's Jubilee.

From the tower, a simple downhill stroll, following Rakehouse Brow, soon brings you back to Lower Lee and Lee Bridge.

Walk 13: Clougha Pike

Start/Finish: Birk Bank Car Park. GR.526604

Distance: 3½ miles (6km). Variant: 6 miles (10km)

Height gain: 965ft (295m). Variant: 1145ft (350m)

Walking time: 2 hours. Variant: 4-4½ hours

Type of Walk: Muddy in places over rough ground, but generally good paths throughout. Recommended for clear summer evenings.

Map: OS Outdoor Leisure Map 41: Forest of Bowland and Ribblesdale

Public transport: HEY operate a service to Quernmore, from where the walk can be started. The Bowland Rambler is also available during summer months.

Grandstand View

This brief outing is truly one of the classics in the Bowland area, and is a popular walk, especially fine on a warm summer's evening when you can perch among the summit rocks and watch the sun go down on Morecambe Bay. Walkers who want a longer walk will find a variant finish that takes in the Jubilee Tower and Brow Top Craft and Farm Visitors Centre.

Clougha Pike lies at the western edge of the Forest of Bowland Area of Outstanding Natural Beauty (AONB) in one of the limited corners of the Area where access is available to walkers. Although little more than thirteen hundred feet in height, Clougha Pike is a splendid hill to visit, and has appeal for a wide range of interests.

The walk begins from the Birk Bank Car Park, not far from the village of Quernmore, leaving the car park at the back corner to follow a wide green track for a short distance to a fork. Turn right, and keep on until you reach another wide green track, and once more turn right. Use a stile to the left of a gate and cross a large expanse of wet ground, aided by a series of duckboards, to another stile at which you can start climbing steadily through woodland.

Clougha Pike

A good track leads on to two more stiles. Use that on the right, and continue steeply up the ensuing field, following the wall to a gate. The path presses on, continuing to climb towards some rocks, rising more gently to reach a wall. Turn right and follow the wall to its end at a large gritstone boulder. You can scramble up a couple of large rocks and go along the escarpment edge to the trig point and shelter on the summit.

The view is surprisingly wide, extending from Blackpool Tower (on a good day) to the fells of Lakeland, with the more obvious urban sprawl of Morecambe and Lancaster closer by. Morecambe Bay is often caught by rays of slanting sunshine, shining silvery beyond the dull-coloured landscape, while the long finger of the River Lune reaches far into the heart of Lancaster, underlining the town's former importance as a trading port with America and beyond.

Return by going along an indistinct track on the other side of the shelter wall. The track improves very soon, and easily descends the steep upper slopes and crosses a stream. To avoid confusion, keep about 70m/yds from a wall on your right, and head down rough

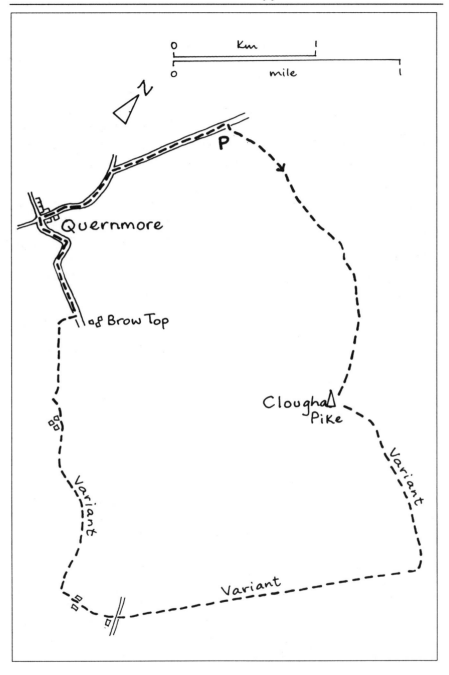

pastures to an Access Land gate. Go through the right-hand of two gates, and down a farm track to Rooten Brook Farm. Keep right between the farm buildings to its main access road. Go down this, cross a stream (the same one you met earlier) and, immediately before a large green shed, go into a walled lane that runs down the side of a wood. You emerge near a house in a hollow.

Head towards the wall corner over on the right, and follow the wall to a gate, there following another access road down to the public road. Turn right, and stroll back to the car park, in about fifteen minutes.

Variant Finish (Round trip: 6 miles/10km: 1145ft/350m) From the summit turn sharply to the right and follow a clear path to a stile. Continue along an undulating path across open moorland marked by a few small cairns. Cross a stile to the right of a fence corner and press on with a wall on your left. This takes you to the highest point of Grit Fell. Here turn right, and descend in a straight line to the Jubilee Tower.

From the tower go down the right-hand side of a wall towards Westfield House Farm. There go along a concrete access track, keeping to the right of the farm buildings, and on through a gate. When the track goes left, leave it and go right, over a stone stile. Keep on across a number of fields by a wall/fence, heading for Hare Appletree Farm. Cross a stream and then follow an undulating path towards the farm, and cross a stile/fence. A short way on go through a gap on the left, cross another stream and then keep on to the hamlet of Hare Appletree.

Head along a surfaced lane between buildings and when the track bends right, go left through a gate (waymark), keeping ahead along a line of trees. When the trees and an adjoining fence end, keep forward, heading obliquely right across a field to a stone stile giving on to another concrete track. Turn right on this to reach the road.

You have a choice here: if you turn right at the road and first left you reach Brow Top Craft and Farm Visitors Centre, always worth a visit. Alternatively, turn left and go down Quernmore Brow to the village crossroads, and there turn right. About 500m/yds along this lane (Rigg Lane), branch right and proceed for a little under half a mile (700m) to return to the car park.

Walk 14: Saddle Fell and Bleadale Water

Start/Finish: Chipping, car park. GR.622433

Distance: 10 miles (16km)

Height gain: 2165ft (660m)

Walking time: 5-6 hours

Type of Walk: A varied and demanding walk, not suited to misty conditions.

Map: OS Outdoor Leisure Map 41: Forest of Bowland and Ribblesdale

Public transport: *Bus:* BBT to Chipping, plus Bowland Wanderer during summer months.

Up and Over, and Back Again

Chipping is a charming retreat of narrow streets, bright cottages, almhouses, old buildings, pubs and an interesting church that announce to the discerning eye that this was once a popular halt on many of the cross-country routes that lace these fells of Bowland.

This walk is made possible by the prolonged and diligent efforts of Lancashire County Council's Countryside Service in negotiating open access areas, and developing with North West Water a series of concessionary pathways. The overall effect is to open up considerably an area that for many years was closed to walkers. There is a small price to pay, however, if you are a dog owner because one of the sticking points in the access agreement areas (other than the bogs) is that dogs are not allowed under any circumstances. My own dogs were greatly aggrieved by this, but had got over it by meal time.

Leave the car park heading towards the church and turn left up the lane. Just over 200m/yds further on, branch right past the chair works, the traditional industry in Chipping. When you reach a mill

Langden Castle, Bowland

pond locate the driveway to a house on the right, just along which the path to Burnslack begins. It is not easy to find.

Having done so, go steeply up-field, then along a fenceline to a stile, keeping above a wooded clough. From the stile a path leads through the woodland to a footbridge. Cross it and head up to Windy Hill Farm, there bearing left on to its access road, and following this out to a surfaced lane below Saddle End.

Cross the road and go along the access past Saddle End Farm to reach a broad track rising on to Saddle Fell. Soon you reach the edge of the Access Area. Once in the Access Area, the track continues to rise, divides, re-joins, but always goes up. There is slightly easier going to the right-hand side of Saddle Fell, and this links in to a better defined track higher up. Keep going in a northerly direction and you will eventually intersect the fence across the watershed. Cross this and keep generally forward to locate the concessionary path leading down into Bleadale. You will find it on the right-hand side of the valley, so take a little time locating it before descending

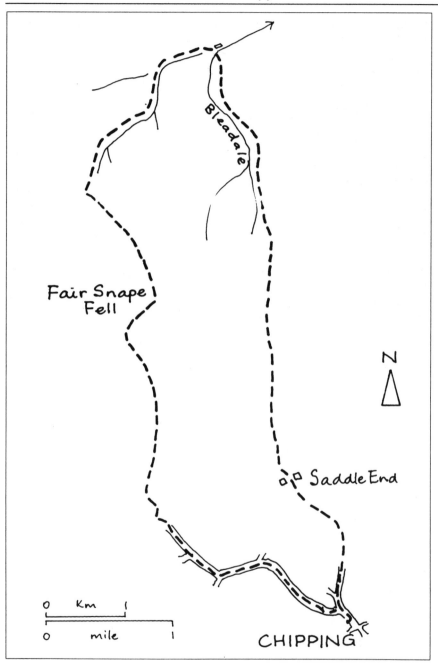

Bleadale

Fair Snape
Fell

N

Saddle End

Km

mile

CHIPPING

too far into Bleadale. The ground is confusing here, which is why I do not advise the walk in poor visibility.

Follow the track down Bleadale Water and it will deliver you directly at the doors of Langden Castle. Cross Langden Brook to reach the 'castle', and turn left. Beyond Langden Castle, a signposted path sets off for Bleasdale. Follow this, and soon you recross Langden Brook.

The on-going path is a little steep for a while, but soon becomes an exciting traverse above the steep-sided ravine of Fiensdale, finally emerging amid a landscape of shallow peat groughs and bedrock. Soon you reach a fence and stile at Fiensdale Head. If now you ignore the stile, but keep to the left of the fence, you travel an agreed a concessionary path up to the summit of Fair Snape Fell, marked by a large cairn.

At Fair Snape Fell, cross the fence by a stile, and follow the on-going fence/wall, first in a south-westerly direction, then east of south and downhill before changing direction slightly once more to reach Parlick. From the top of Parlick you follow an obvious path down to Fell Foot. From Fell Foot, walk down the lane to a junction. Keep ahead to to T-junction with Fish House Lane. Keep right at the next junction and you can follow pleasant lanes all the way back to Chipping, but do take care against traffic. Although these are 'quiet' country lanes, 'quiet' is a relative thing, and the roads well used.

Walk 15: Parlick and Fair Snape Fell

Start/Finish: Fell Foot, reached from Chipping. GR.599446

Distance: 7½ miles (12km)

Height gain: 1000ft (305m)

Walking time: 3-4 hours

Type of Walk: A steep start, but otherwise easy. No dogs. Not recommended in poor visibility.

Map: OS Outdoor Leisure Map 41: Forest of Bowland and Ribblesdale

Public transport: *Bus:* BBT run a service to Chipping; plus the Bowland Wanderer from May to September.

Very Fair Indeed

In spite of a steep start this short tour of Parlick and Fair Snape Fell is very popular and enjoyable. Throughout the walk there are good views that embrace the entire coastal plain of Lancashire, the Lakeland Fells across Morecambe Bay and the central summits of the Pennines.

The walk begins from Fell Foot, a restored house literally, as its name suggests, at the foot of Parlick, but it should be preceded or followed by a visit to the nearby village of Chipping. Here is a snug, self-contained community with narrow streets flanked by ancient cottages and inns that tell of the village's importance in years gone by as a staging post for travellers.

Parking is limited at Fell Foot itself, but where the access road leaves the "main" road, at a sharp bend, there is a small parking area. It is important also to note that the walk goes through the Fairsnape Access Area within which dogs are not allowed, on or off leads.

Walk up the lane to Fell Foot, go through the gate and immediately

Almshouses and old school, Chipping

start up the constructed pathway beyond. This soon eases to a more acceptable gradient, keeping left of a broad gully. A steady plod soon brings the top of Parlick into view. Cross the fence along the summit by a stile, and follow it, descending slightly, crossing a shallow col and a minor bump en route, before climbing again, now in the company of a wall. Continue on a broad trail, moving gradually away from the wall as it heads towards the southern edge of Fair Snape Fell and crossing another fence on the way.

The top of Fair Snape Fell is a massive plateau, crowned by a large cairn, a shelter and trig pillar. The view is excellent. To the north-west Morecambe Bay is backed by the dark form of Black Combe, spreading right along the line of the central Lakeland fells. On a good day, usually in winter, the Isle of Man can be seen just to the left of Black Combe: To the south rises the distant bulk of Winter Hill, Great Hill and, much nearer, Beacon Fell. Further to the south-east the distant Pennine summits ease into view beyond Pendle Hill, while directly below, the quilted fields of rural Lancashire at its best ripple outwards.

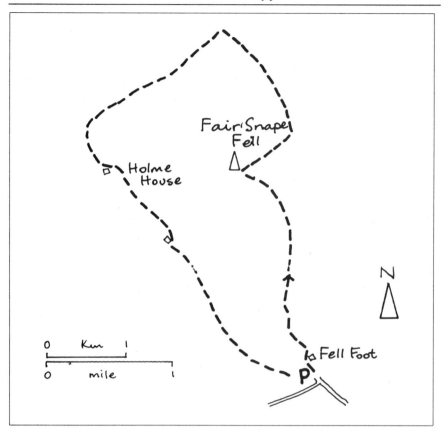

This summit, however, does not mark the highest point of Fair
Snape Fell. To reach this, visible a short distance away, walk
towards a wall corner, where the wall abuts a fence. Cross the fence,
and set off through a sea of peat hags and small hummocks, usually
dry, to reach the cairn topped by a post that does mark the top of
the fell. Away to the right rises Totridge, while far away, left,
Hawthornthwaite Fell Top rises beyond the dip that locates
Fiendsdale.

Cross the fence at this point and go left along it for almost a mile
(1.5km) to a stile where the path from Fiensdale rises from the right
to continue its journey to Bleasdale. Now go left, over the stile, and
descend obliquely across the southern slopes of Bleasdale Fell. As

the gradient eases the path changes direction, going through a gate in a wall, and continues descending across fields to reach Holme House Farm. Go past the farm into a walled lane, but as this starts to swing towards Vicarage Farm, leave it, branching left on an improving path that becomes a track leading to Higher Fair Snape Farm.

Go through the farm, and past two houses. Follow the on-going lane, but as you approach the obvious dell containing the infant River Brock, leave the track and go through a gate on the left. Cross two streams and walk up the field opposite to a gate giving on to another track. Turn right, cross another stream, and then go steeply uphill to a stile giving on to a rough track. Look for a green pathway slanting up the slopes of Parlick and follow this to reach the edge of the Access Area. Cross a stile, turn left with a fence to another stile, another stream and a large pasture, at the end of which you reach a massive set of stone steps – quite some stile – over a wall. Go downhill a little to a stile near a small woodland, and then keep across the next field to a ladder stile, from which you descend to a gate giving on to the lane to Fell Foot.

Walk 16: Whitendale and Croasdale

Start/Finish: Slaidburn, car park by the river. GR.714523

Distance: 12 miles (13km)

Height gain: 1590ft (485 metres)

Walking time: 5-6 hours

Type of Walk: Involving two ascents, though neither is arduous, the effort of this walk is easily outweighed by the sheer beauty of this isolated corner of Lancashire.

Map: OS Outdoor Leisure 41: Forest of Bowland and Ribblesdale

Public transport: *Bus:* HYN operate a bus service between Clitheroe and Settle that goes to Slaidburn, plus Bowland Rambler and Bowland Pathfinder – May to September.

Into the Heart of Bowland

Though it is rather better known now than of old, walkers who want a taste of solitude should visit the lonely valley of Whitendale. Do so not by the tame access road that probes northwards from Dunsop Bridge, but over the hill of Dunsop Fell, for it is then that the vision of the emerald and fertile pastures hidden among this tightly enclosed sanctum springs upon you with a suddenness that is as captivating as it is startling. Here is an enchanting, almost forgotten world, a sanctum of peace and quiet, where green fields offer a stark contrast to the sombre hills all around. I included this walk in the first book in this series *50 Classic Walks in the Pennines*. The quality of the walk is such that I can think of no justifiable reason for excluding it from this collection: it is unquestionably one of Lancashire's finest.

The day begins in the village of Slaidburn, the former administrative capital of the Forest of Bowland. Leave the car park and turn right to climb past the war memorial and the Hark to Bounty Inn. Continue ahead for 1½ km (1 mile) to a road (Wood House Lane) that goes to the right. Ignore this lane and continue for another 300m/yds to a rough farm track on the right, leaving the road after a bend, at GR.693531. Ahead is the solitary building of Burn Side, to the right of which the track heads for wild country. Now the steepness of Dunsop Fell awaits, tackled by the narrow ridge separating the lower ground just crossed and a narrow, steep-sided valley, Dunsop Brook, beyond.

As more level ground is reached, the path swings north-west across the top of Dunsop Brook. A short distance further, near the

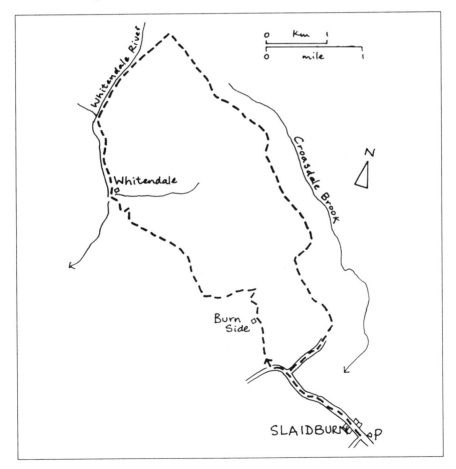

highest point of Dunsop Fell, you cross a narrow mossy-banked stream, with a wall coming in from the left. Gradually move towards the wall to a concealed gate at Dunsop Head, a fine vantage point, and a good place for a breather. The apparent close proximity of other Bowland hills is surprising: Totridge rises to the south with Fair Snape Fell's sweeping ridge rolling away complacently behind it. Further north lie Ward's Stone and Wolfhole Crag.

From Dunsop Head to Whitendale Farm the route has been waymarked by the water authority, and continues for a while on more or less level ground before descending with the mound of Middle Knoll ahead and left, separating the valleys of Whitendale and Brennand. To the left of Middle Knoll, the rivers of the two valleys unite to flow as one, Dunsop River, south to join the River Hodder at Dunsop Bridge.

Approaching Whitendale Farm the path threads a carpet of heather, the route pinned in place by stone cairns and waymarking posts. Finally, by a grouse-shooters' track, you reach the farm. Go through the yard with the buildings to your right, and then turn right at a junction to cross a bridged tributary which puts Whitendale River on your left. Now head north with the line of the river, past a bridge (do not cross it) to a forked pathway beyond a gate, and there keep left. The path begins to climb as you head for Hornby Road, a salt packhorse route of uncertain date, better known as the Salter Fell track. Still you climb, and after passing through newish plantations, the ground becomes less even.

Higher up the path also becomes less distinct, but keep the river nearby and watch for a cairn that in summer is concealed by ferns; shortly afterwards you ford a stream. Now is the time to abandon the stream, though still heading in much the same direction, and to tackle a fairly rough section (still waymarked by posts) until Hornby Road is reached.

To the left the track heads for Hornby in the Lune valley, but your route goes to the right, roughly following the course of Croasdale Brook, but remaining high above it. Keep on past quarry workings on the shoulder of Baxton Fell, and lower down cross Black Brook at New Bridge. This old road speeds you down, around Low Fell, to a five-barred gate, and beyond to join the upper section of Wood House Lane, by which an easy return is made to Slaidburn.

Walk 17: Stocks Reservoir Circuit

Start/Finish: Slaidburn car park. GR.713524

Distance: 9 miles (14.5km)

Height gain: 320ft (100m)

Walking time: 4-5 hours

Type of Walk: Easy, with one (usually) easy river crossing.

Map: OS Outdoor Leisure Map 41: Forest of Bowland and Ribblesdale

Public transport: *Bus:* HYN to Slaidburn, plus Bowland Rambler and Bowland Pathfinder May to September.

By Wood and Water

Stocks Reservoir lies to the north of Slaidburn, from where it makes a splendid circuit in spring and early summer. This circuit is quite long, but the walking is easy. Be sure to take plenty of refreshments. Slaidburn, about which I have written more in Walk 21, used to be the administrative centre for the ancient Forest of Bowland, and the former courtroom used to be part of the Hark to Bounty Inn. There is a relaxed, unhurried air about the village, in spite of the sometimes overbearing attentions of weekend visitors.

Start from the car park in Slaidburn and turn right to the War Memorial, there going right again. Once across Croasdale Brook, turn right into a field and head for a wall at the far side which steers you to a track that takes you (right) to cross the River Hodder. Beyond the river you trek up to Hammerton Hall, a fine Elizabethan house.

Keep on to farm buildings and branch right to three gates. Choose the left gate, and pursue a line of yellow waymarks past Black House and out along the access road to the road at St James's Church. Turn left up the road to the Gisburn Forest car park (an alternative starting point), with a few opportunities to wander in and out of forest.

Go through the car park on to a number of waymarked trails (red and white), and follow these until you discover a yellow waymark (about ten minutes or so). Having found it, ignore it, and keep straight on. In a few minutes you reach a clearing. Branch left and a few more minutes will bring you out of the forest, and soon crossing Hasgill Beck.

A good track leads to the ruins of New House, shortly before which turn left through a gate, soon reaching a walled lane. Turn left, and in a minute or so go right through a gate into a field. Turn right and follow the wall to a gate, beyond which a wide green track leads you down to the ford at the River Hodder. If you don't like the thought of crossing the river (seldom a real problem), the map shows an alternative loop up towards Catlow, crossing the river at Lock Bridge

War Memorial, Slaidburn

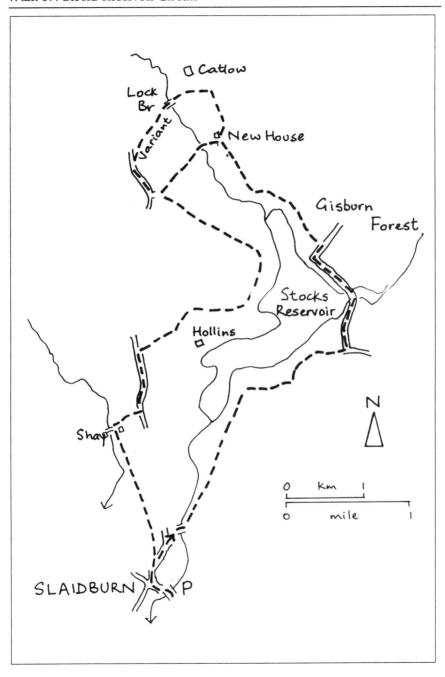

(GR.713584) and rejoining the original line a short distance south of Kenibus, at a road corner.

Once across the ford, cross a field to a gate and keep on to Collyholme. Go through a large gap in a wall on the left, then follow a stream and a couple of stiles. This way brings you to a wide green track and a gate. Beyond the gate, leave the track and bear right through rushes. Another green track materialises beyond, and soon proves to be an old railway trackbed, used to bring stone from a nearby quarry. Follow the track for 1½ miles (waymarked, yellow) until it starts to pass a hollow, where a footpath sign marks the point at which to leave it.

Go uphill, near woodland, past a barn ruin to another barn. Go past the ruins, and in a hollow you find a clear path that leads you over a shoulder, across a stream by a simple bridge, then bears left to woodland. Cross a stile, bearing half left to a waymark post, then go down the field to the track leading to Hollins House. Turn right along the track to reach the road. Go left down the road, which you can stay with back to Slaidburn, but do take care since the road is quite busy in summer. Alternatively, you need only follow the road as far as the track to Shay House, and here turn right to approach Croasdale Brook. Just before the brook, go left over a stile into a field, the first of many (with stiles) that lead you always in much the same direction, back towards the road, which you meet just a short way out of Slaidburn. Turn right, continuing down to cross Croasdale Beck on the edge of Slaidburn, and then go left as you enter the village to return, past the Hark to Bounty, to the car park.

Walk 18: Slaidburn and the River Hodder

Start/Finish: Slaidburn car park. GR.713524

Distance: 7 miles (12km)

Height gain: A few ups and downs, but nothing serious.

Walking time: 2½-3 hours

Type of Walk: Delightful rural walking, mainly on clear paths and tracks.

Maps: The OS Outdoor Leisure Map 41: Forest of Bowland and Ribblesdale covers part of the walk; OS Pathfinder Sheet 660: Slaidburn and Forest of Bowland covers all the walk

Public transport: *Bus:* HYN to Slaidburn, plus Bowland Rambler and Bowland Pathfinder – May to September.

Around Slaidburn Pastures

This walk begins, if you need a precise beginning, at the Hark to Bounty Inn in Slaidburn, a fine compact village with a church founded in 1246 and rebuilt in the fifteenth century, which is notable for its Jacobean triple-decker pulpit and chancel screen.

Jessica Lofthouse, in *Lancashire Villages,* describes Slaidburn, the administrative centre for the forest of Bowland, as "perfect ... [lying] snugly in a deep hollow you must always climb to get in or out of the village exciting heather-clad fells above and pure enchantment in the lush green meadows and pastures below".

The inn, which dates from the thirteenth century, was, until 1895 (some say 1875), known simply as The Dog. Then the parson, Wigglesworth, also the local squire, called in for refreshment one day while out with his hounds. From amid the baying and barking of the assembled hounds outside the squire is said to have detected the voice of his favourite hound, exclaiming, "Hark to Bounty!" The

Hark to Bounty Inn, Slaidburn

inn also used to house the ancient courtroom of the Forest of Bowland, which was still in use until 1937, and is said to have been used by Oliver Cromwell.

Anyway, if you dwell overlong as you reach the inn, you may find you go no further, but that would never do. Far better to stride off on an invigorating walk, and then avail yourself of the inn's services on the return.

So, go past the pub and progressively out of the village, staying on the road for about a mile. Then turn down the driveway to Parrock Head Hotel, and go through the car park in front of the building, a converted farmhouse, and through a gate at the end. Turn right before reaching a barn. Continue through a field gate and move towards the wall on the right, heading for a stile at the top of the field. Beyond, stay close by the wall until it bends right. Then cross the field to the white building of Laythams.

Pass through a gate on the right and then go left along the road. Within a few strides take a gate on the right, and aim half left across

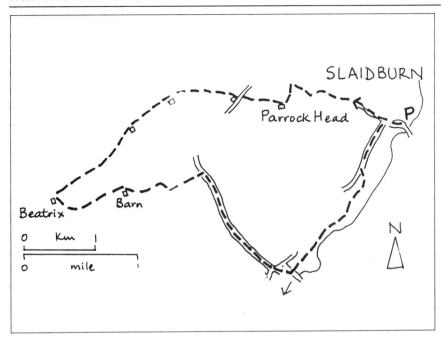

the ensuing field, heading west towards Burn House Farm, your next objective. You'll encounter a number of stiles and fields on the way, but you can just see the farm buildings, and they will keep you in the right direction. I seem to recall that it was on this walk that I discovered quite a few small fossils in the limestone walls; you might find them, too, but don't expect dinosaur bones, just tiny crinoids.

Go behind the farm on a surfaced lane, and follow this for about half a mile, past The Hey and below the swelling slopes of Burn Fell. As the lane bends to pass through an old fence (look for a single gatepost), go through a gate on the right and along a fence and ditch to the end of the field, to enter woodland ahead. Go between trees and downhill to a small gate; it's all rather squelchy for a while, and not always clear which way to go, so stay alert for this stretch, otherwise I may lose you forever! Beyond the gate you cross a stream and clamber up a steep slope on a narrow path. At the top of the slope, cross moorland, with a fence on your right, to reach a farm access, near Beatrix Farm. Go left through the farmyard, and soon take a left-hand trail rising easily upwards. When this trail passes some hawthorns, aim a little to the left until a barn comes into view, and then head for it. Keep the barn on your right, and trend left across a field to a gate. Press on downhill, cross a stream, and then climb on a track past Rough Syke Barn to a gate.

Beyond the gate you reach another track, Bull Lane. Follow this out to reach the roadway, and turn right, walking the road to the village of Newton. It's all very pleasant, but do take care with traffic. Go down the road (towards Clitheroe) and past the Parkers Arms to a double-arched bridge over the River Hodder. Do not cross the bridge, but go left just before it, upstream for a short distance and then through a gate giving access to a stone track beside the river. You leave the river for a time, keeping ahead beside a wall. Cross a bridge on the right, and a stile, and then turn left, now with a stream on your left. Head for the wooded hillside of Great Dunmow, following a path through the woods. Keep on, through a kissing gate and across a field, with Dunmow Hall appearing on your left. A rough track takes you past the Hall and round the base of more woodland, eventually to reach the road between Newton and Slaidburn. When you do, turn right, and stroll back to Slaidburn – the Hark to Bounty awaits.

Walk 19: Dunsop Head and Whitendale

Start/Finish: Dunsop Bridge. GR.661501

Distance: 10 miles (16km)

Height gain: 1395ft (425m)

Walking time: 5-6 hours

Type of Walk: A long and demanding walk across high, isolated moorlands. Not recommended in poor visibility.

Map: OS Outdoor Leisure Map 41: Forest and Bowland and Ribblesdale

Public transport: *Bus:* HYN operate a service to Dunsop Bridge. In addition there is the Leisure Link service: Bowland Rambler, Ribble Valley Rambler and Bowland Pathfinder.

Out by Hodder: Back by Dunsop

This walk visits some of the remoter parts of the Forest of Bowland and is an energetic walk for experienced walkers only. It begins from the car park in Dunsop Bridge, a small village focused around an attractive hump-backed bridge over the river from which it takes its name.

Leave the car park and turn left along the road for little more than 100m/yds, and as the road bends left, leave it, right, for a footpath (signposted) along the drive to Thorneyholme Hall. Before this driveway crosses the River Hodder, go left through a gate and take to a path across a field, heading for a small woodland. The route passes through this woodland and continues beside the Hodder to reach a road near Boarsden. Turn right and walk along the road for about 500m/yds to a stile on the left. Cross this and continue in a north-easterly direction to reach another lane near Brown Hills. Turn left along the lane for 400m/yds, and then leave it, turning right, along the access track to Crawshaw Farm.

Head towards the farm, going to the left of it, and continue beside a wall, eventually to reach and follow a track to Pain Hill Farm. Here turn right around a barn to a stile. Onward the route continues to descend to cross a stream before rising a little to reach Parrock Head Hotel. Walk out from the hotel, a former farmhouse, along its drive to a lane and there turn left along the road. Leave the road after a bend, at GR.693531, and head for the solitary cottage of Burn Side, passing to the right of it as the track heads for wild country.

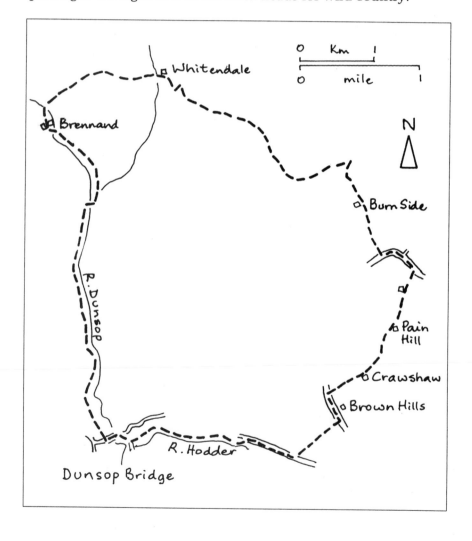

The steep slopes of Dunsop Fell are eased by a narrow ridge separating the ground just crossed and the steep-sided valley of Dunsop Brook beyond. When the gradient eases, the path curves north-west across the top of Dunsop Brook. A short way on, near the top of Dunsop Fell, you cross a narrow mossy-banked stream, near a wall. Gradually head for the wall to locate a concealed gate at Dunsop Head, an outstanding viewpoint.

From Dunsop Head to Whitendale Farm the route is waymarked, and presses on for a while on more or less level ground before descending, with the mound of Middle Knoll ahead and left separating the valleys of Whitendale and Brennand.

Approaching Whitendale Farm the path follows stone cairns and waymarking posts, and finally reaches the farm. Here pass through the yard, and turn right at a junction to cross a bridged tributary which puts Whitendale River on our left. Now head steeply up-wards, crossing the shoulder of Middle Knoll to a gate. Beyond the gate turn left by a wall, and after about 50m/yds turn right on a well-trodden pathway to a stile. Beyond the stile keep on in a roughly south-westerly direction, descending easily to reach Brennand Farm, crossing Brennand River on the way.

Beyond the farm a bridleway runs on to recross the river, then to Lower Brennand and eventually to the confluence between the Brennand and Whitendale rivers. The route runs into the apex of the confluence before crossing what is about to become the River Dunsop at a bridge. Easy walking now ensues as you pursue the Dunsop roughly southwards, recrossing it, and finally easing out of this delightful valley to return to Dunsop Bridge.

Walk 20: Nicky Nook and Grize Dale

Start/Finish: Scorton. GR.502487

Distance: 6 miles (9.5km)

Height gain: 400ft (130m)

Walking time: 3 hours

Type of Walk: A fairly easy walk, with superb views.

Map: OS Outdoor Leisure Map 41: Forest of Bowland and Ribblesdale

Public transport: *Bus:* RIB operate services between Scorton and Garstang.

Finishing Touch

Far from being a hidden corner, Nicky Nook stands high above the Wyre and Calder valleys, a last glorious finishing touch of paint on the canvas that is the Forest of Bowland. To the west the Lancashire coastal plain slips out to the sea along the Fylde coast, while to the east, its higher siblings of the Forest form a burgeoning upland of heathery moorland, a stark contrast to the flatlands of Fylde. Between the two, the former primary route north-south, the A6, has lost much of its importance to the main West Coast railway line and the noisy, bustling activity of the M6 motorway. But on Nicky Nook, you are high above all this, in a world plainly there for everyone to see, but invariably ignored by other than the most discerning.

If you drive through Scorton, you should find room to park (limited) close by the place where the path over Nicky Nook leaves the back road junction of Snow Hill Lane and Higher Lane. A better option would be to take the bus from Garstang, or to park at the picnic area about a mile north of Scorton and to begin the walk from there.

Scorton is one of Lancashire's most charming villages, and boasts three churches: Roman Catholic, Anglican and Methodist, all of Victorian origin. It is a thriving community, and centres on its village school, which has been educating new generations of Scorton children for more than a hundred years. Like neighbouring villages of Dolphinholme and Caldervale, Scorton is one of Lancashire's earliest mill villages, developed when two brothers, the

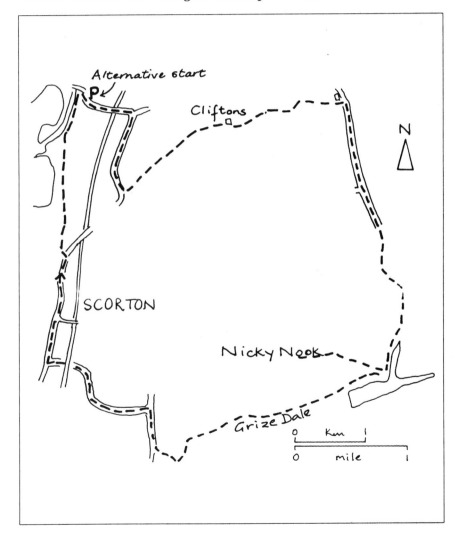

Fishwicks, arrived from Burnley in 1809 to start a factory using village labour. Now all the workers' homes have been converted, and many of the attractive thatched cottages that stood here are gone.

Head north out of Scorton, on the road signposted to the Trough of Bowland, but only for about a quarter of a mile, to a signposted footpath on the left, about 50m/yds before the road crosses the motorway. A series of pastures, accessed by stiles, now leads you northwards as you approach Scorton Lake and Cleveleymere, and the picnic site and nature trail near Ashbournes.

Just before the picnic site, turn right along a road which leads you across the motorway, and turn right again at a T-junction, continuing down the road back towards Scorton. Before reaching a bridge over Park Brook, cross a stile on the left and court the brook via footbridges and stiles until the path bears right, near a pond. By a stile in a field corner you reach a quiet lane. Cross it, and another stile to enter a field beyond, now heading for the farm at Cliftons.

Go through the farmyard, leaving via a gate near the house, and ascend by a fence to a stile. Keep on, across fields, to reach Sykes Farm. Beyond the farm you reach a track. Turn right along it and soon join a lane, which you follow to reach a ford. Beyond the ford the lane rises towards Grize Dale. Ignore the turning to Scorton, but keep ahead to go through a gate to enter Grize Dale and so reach its reservoir, one of three that cluster in this delightful, hidden valley.

Grizedale Reservoir is pleasantly wooded, and quite unsuspected by passers-by on the north-south routes to the east. As you reach the reservoir, turn right, and soon, at a point where the track bends sharply, cross a stile and take a prominent path that ascends in a north-westerly direction to reach the top of Nicky Nook, an amazingly good vantage point for so lowly a summit.

To continue, simply retrace your steps to the reservoir, turn right, and pursue a broad track until, near Pedder's Wood, you can turn right at a footbridge, heading for the Wood. Soon you join Higher Lane, not far from Slean End. If you go right and left after about 250m/yds, you descend Tithe Barn Lane and so return to Scorton village.

Walk 21: Beacon Fell and the River Brock

Start/Finish: Carwags car park and picnic site, south-east of the country park. GR.578423

Distance: 7 miles (12km)

Height gain: 675ft (205m)

Walking time: 3-3½ hours

Type of Walk: Easy woodland and riverside walking on good paths.

Maps: OS Outdoor Leisure Map 41: Forest of Bowland and Ribblesdale

Public transport: *Bus:* Beacon Fell Country Park is served by the Bowland Pathfinder summer service.

Beacon Bounds

Lying within the Forest of Bowland Area of Outstanding Natural Beauty, Beacon Fell comprises 75 hectares (185 acres) of rough moorland and woodland, designated as a country park in 1969. It lies 8 miles north of Preston, and is signposted from Broughton, from Brock Bridge, and from Longridge. The park is managed by Lancashire's Countryside Service, and provides an excellent oasis of escape from every-day troubles. At weekends especially, Beacon Fell is very popular.

This walk begins from the Carwags Car Park and Picnic Area at the south-eastern edge of the country park, where if you wish you can also arrange a barbecue. From the corner of the car park, set off along a path (signposted to the summit of Beacon Fell) that runs between a fence and the road. When you meet the end of a wall, go right, keeping the wall on your left, and following a broad track through sparse woodland. When the path forks, keep left, and continue, to meet another road at a constructed gap through a wall.

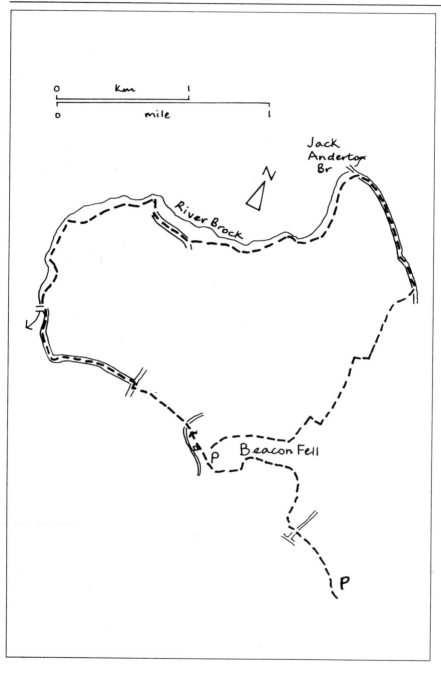

Cross the road and follow a path, covered with wood chippings, until you meet a wide, graded track running left-right. Go left here and follow the track to a waymark at a meeting of pathways. Cross a small bridge on the right, and follow a straight path along the edge of woodland, ignoring intermediate pathways, until you reach the Quarry Wood Car Park.

Here, take a prominent, ascending path, left, running away from the car park, and rising gradually and rockily, to a boggy plateau. Keep ahead, and at a fork, go right, to follow an improving path, gradually bringing the trig pillar on the summit of Beacon Fell into view. Continue to the summit, which has a splendid view of the surrounding countryside of Lancashire.

Leave the summit by going left on another broad track, though there are many options if you are willing to explore. At the first crossroads, keep ahead, descending, until you reach a track at which you can go right, to the Fell House Car Park, picnic area, toilets, and information centre.

Go past the picnic area to a path, turn left along it and keep going until you reach a road. Cross the road and go along the path opposite to a stile. Cross it and start descending steeply, heading for a small plantation ahead. Keep going down, and crossing stiles until you reach another road. Turn right and then take the first turning on the left, White Lee Lane. Follow this until you encounter the River Brock at Higher Brock Bridge.

Do not cross the bridge, but keep forward to a stile near the access to Brock Cottage Farm. Cross the stile and head slightly left, on a track, towards the farm buildings, and then turn right, by a fenceline, and when this ends keep ahead to reach the river. Now follow the river through its delightful wooded valley to a weir, there leaving the river for a short while by a path heading right, to join a track. Turn left along the track, but after a few strides go right on a path that trends leftwards below a wooded embankment and soon rejoins the river. Now stay with the river as far as a footbridge. There turn right on a stony track (Snape Rake Lane) for about 350m/yds, leaving it at a pair of old gateposts on the left. Very soon you rejoin the river once more, and stay in its company, more or less, for about one mile (1.5km), until you descend to reach a road near Jack Anderson Bridge.

Here turn right and follow the road to Higher Brock Mill, now a post office and café. Follow the road as it bends and starts to climb, and near the top turn right, up steps, to a stile. Cross the stile and keep along the left edge of a field to another stile, before heading for Wickins Barn Farm. Go through the farmyard to a road. Turn right, and about 100m/yds after a sharp right bend leave the road at a signposted footpath (farm access), and keep forward for about 400m/yds. When the track bends left, leave it by a waymarked stile, and follow a rising path that leads you back to the road that encircles Beacon Fell.

At the road turn right and immediately left on an ascending path through conifers. Cross a track and an open area before returning to the conifers to return to the picnic area and information centre.

Walk away from the information centre, across the car park, to follow a rising cobbled pathway. At the top of the climb keep ahead, now descending through woodland once more. Just before you reach a road, and after a small bridge over a stream, go left into woodland once more, following a good path to meet a broad trail encountered on the outward section of the walk. Now simply retrace your steps to the Carwags Car Park.

Walk 22: Along the Ribble from Ribchester

Start/Finish: Ribchester car park. GR.650354

Distance: 5 miles (8km)

Height gain: Nominal

Walking time: 2½-3 hours

Type of Walk: Quite historical, so allow time to see and visit places; otherwise very pastoral. The great number of stiles followed by fields and by yet more stiles is less confusing than it sounds.

Map: OS Pathfinder Sheet 680: Longridge and Great Harwood

Public transport: *Bus:* RIB and DCS operate services that link Ribchester with Preston and Blackburn.

By Ribble Banks

Ironically, I live only a few minutes from the River Ribble, but rarely get a chance to walk beside it. The whole of the River Ribble is one of which Lancastrians are proud, and this short walk makes the most of the area around the town of Ribchester, which grew from, or rather on, a Roman fort constructed during the first century, known as Bremetennacum. Part of the fort lies beneath the 13th-century church, close by which the Roman Museum is well worth your time.

Start from the main car park, go left to a T-junction and then right, to go past the White Bull pub. Note the eighteenth century cottages opposite the pub. They once housed the handloom weavers who figured in an industry that occupied many of the villages in this part of Lancashire for years. The White Bull was originally built as the local courthouse and is of uncertain original date; the datestone of 1707 relates to a subsequent rebuilding. The porch of the pub makes use of Roman pillars that were salvaged from the Ribble.

Go up Water Street, turning right at a crossroads. Just after the

Ribchester Arms, go left along Stydd Lane. Keep to the right of an attractive group of almshouses (endowed in 1726 for Catholic women), cross a bridge over a stream and just before reaching Stydd Chapel (also worthy of your attention), turn left on to a grassy path beside a stream. Go left over a footbridge, and right to a stile. Cross a field to another stile and on along an enclosed path to yet another stile, beyond which one more stile brings you on to a lane.

Turn left to a 30mph road sign, and there go right on a farm access track. Keep the farm buildings to your right as you approach them,

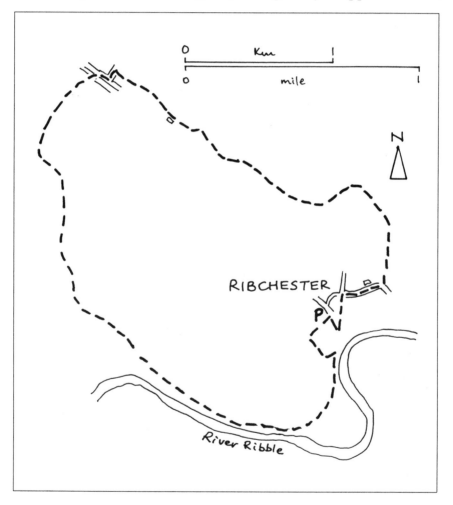

and keep going to a house. Go in front of the house, turning right as you pass the end of it, and instantly left through a gate. Keep ahead over a field to a fence, and, keeping the fence on your left, head downhill to a footbridge.

Cross the bridge and follow the stream into a sheltered valley to another footbridge. An uphill path guides you through trees to a stile, beyond which you cross another field to a farm. When you reach the end of the field, go along a track ahead in front of attractive Buckley Hall. After about 100m/yds turn right at a stile, and half left to slant steeply downhill towards an old mill building. Cross a stile and keep on downhill to another, then go left along a path to pass the mill, and along a drive to reach a lane.

Climb left to a T-junction, and turn right along a road for a mere 50m/yds or so, then go left through a gate. Trend right to the field margin, and keep along the right hand field edge. Cross a ditch by a footbridge and go over the next field to a stile, and then bear left to cross another footbridge, another stream. In the next field continue to a stile and then head for a ruined barn, where you reach a track. Cross the track, and a stile, and keep ahead across the field, downhill to yet another footbridge in the left hand corner.

Over this footbridge you start climbing again by a line of trees and a fence to a stile, then turning left across the ensuing field to locate another, less obvious, stile near a ditch. Go straight across the next field to another stile and turn right along the edge of the field that follows (fence), and move left to reach a grassy track. Turn right, through a gate, and in a few strides left to a stile.

Now you are moving above a narrow, wooded dean on your left, to reach the ten millionth stile of the walk! Keep ahead to the left of a small copse, where you will discover, providing you've found your way to the correct copse, a fine view of the Ribble valley.

Go downhill to go through a gate, where you join the Ribble Way, a fine walk, well documented in the late Gladys Sellers' book. Now you can enjoy a riverside path above the Ribble, keeping on until the track becomes enclosed by hedges that will steer you back to Ribchester. As you go you can ponder the daring of early travellers who used to cross the river at this point; you have only to gauge its width and study the strength behind those stately-flowing waters to realise quite how audacious such an undertaking was.

Walk 23: Longridge Fell

Start/Finish: Lay-by near Hurst Green village. GR.687380

Distance: 6¼ miles (10km)

Height gain: 820ft (250m)

Walking time: 3-4 hours

Type of Walk: Moderate; some uphill and moorland walking. Generally good paths, but muddy at times. Wear stout walking boots and warm clothing.

Map: OS Pathfinders 669: Clitheroe and Chipping, and 680: Longridge and Great Harwood

Public transport: *Bus:* BPT operate services to Hurst Green from Clitheroe and Longridge.

A Green and Pleasant Land

Commanding a fine view northwards across the Hodder valley and that of the lesser River Loud to the Bowland fells, Longridge Fell, in spite of its cloak of dark woodland, remains a place of popular resort with Lancashire countrygoers. This pleasant approach begins in the village of Hurst Green, to the south of the fell, sitting astride Dean Brook whose waters flow briefly to unite with the River Ribble.

The village of Hurst Green lies on the north side of the River Ribble. Jessica Lofthouse comments that the village "deep in its Dean, or flung high on a breezy hillside, from Macadam's dignified new road of 1822 to the park gate of Stonyhurst, shows a pleasant face to all comers". It was visited by Oliver Cromwell and his army of Ironsides in August 1648. They camped at nearby Stonyhurst Park as he passed through to take on the Royalist army at Walton Bridge near Preston. Hurst Green is unquestionably an attractive and comely settlement, much sought after by off-comers and those who, in the wake of tourism, sought out country places to live.

For many years the main industry here was farming, but the village's prosperity began to grow significantly when Sir Nicholas Sherburne (or Shireburn) of Stonyhurst Hall had his tenants taught the skills of spinning and weaving, even keeping rooms in his hall

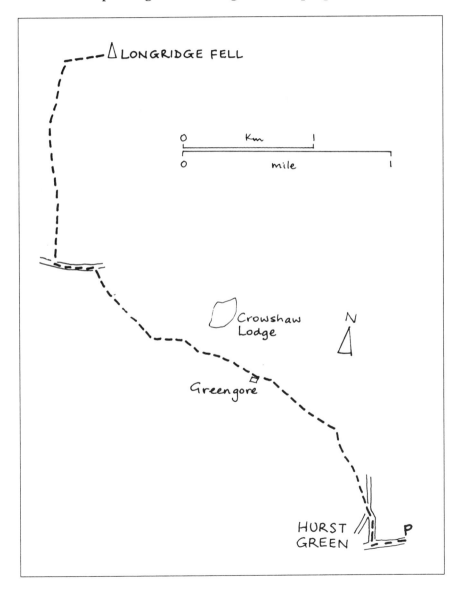

for "as many as could spare time from their families" to become proficient. Nor did his generosity stop there for he provided every-one with yarn and looms "whereby the countryside around began to prosper" and the village became full of "busy little mills, rows of workers' cottages, and the sound of rushing water".

The Sherburnes were lords of the manor from the 1370s until 1717, when the estate changed hands and became very neglected. In 1791 the house was offered to the Society of Jesus, who over many years turned it into one of the foremost boarding schools for boys of the Roman Catholic faith.

Begin from a lay-by on the B6243 Longridge-Clitheroe road, on the Clitheroe side of Hurst Green. Go into the village, and turn right opposite the Shireburn Arms, and walk up the road to the Bayley Arms. There, almost opposite, turn down a lane on the left to reach some garages. Go past them on the right to a road that passes a house and continues into woodland. Soon you can join a cart track, which is often muddy after rain, that goes right through the woods to cross a bridge, beyond which the way is along an agreeable green lane. When the lane meets a farm access, bear right and go past Greengore, beyond which the path becomes grassy once more.

When you leave the woodland behind, the path follows a wall and becomes wet again for a while. As Longridge Fell hoves into view, so you reach a stile and then some redundant gateposts. Above them, between trees, you can make out another stile. Head for it, and once over it, go diagonally right to a stile spanning a fence in a field corner. Keep going then to reach a road.

Turn left along the road for about 400m/yds until you can turn right up a rough track. Keep up this track until it turns to Moor Game Hall. Keep ahead here, the green lane soon degenerating to a footpath which you now simply follow up the moorland slopes to cross a forestry road. Shortly you reach the wall along the ridge of Longridge Fell and a splendid view northwards to the fells of Bowland. You can return from this point if you wish, but the highest point of Longridge Fell lies a few minutes walk away to the right. Once there simply retrace your steps.

Walk 24: Pendle Hill from the Nick of Pendle

Start/Finish: Nick of Pendle, north-west of Sabden village. GR.771385. Limited parking

Distance: 6½ miles (10.5km)

Height gain: 835ft (255m)

Walking time: Allow 3-4 hours

Type of Walk: Ideal for a cold clear day in autumn; little more than an elevated stroll over moorland, but could be confusing in mist.

Map: OS Outdoor Leisure Map 41: Forest of Bowland and Ribblesdale

Public transport: *Bus:* Leisure Link: the Pendle Witch Hopper, in addition to which LAK operate a service between Clitheroe and Sabden.

Slumbering Sentinel

Once described as a living creature stretched in sleep, the great sleek whaleback of Pendle Hill so dominates the surrounding countryside that it was once credited with far greater height than it really has. It has long been a deservedly popular hill walk with the people of Lancashire.

This whole area, of course, is steeped in tales of the Pendle witches, a rather complex, seemingly unjust (in some cases) episode in English history, when witchcraft, being in league with the Devil, was a popular explanation for misfortune. Significantly, it was not sufficient for witches to be condemned; they had to be identified as agents of the Devil, and ironically quite a few of them confessed to such association. Presumably they took the view that by living up to expectations they maintained a certain status within their community, even if it meant death. The confessions, which today we might look upon as fictions of a deranged mind, were always treated seriously, even though judges became increasingly sceptical. Indeed, during the seventeenth century it became quite difficult to find a judge who would convict someone on charges of witchcraft.

As a rule, witches were from the poorer elements of the community, though Alice Nutter, one of 19 witches brought to trial in Lancaster in 1612, was described as a rich woman with a sizeable estate. Modern historians, however, tend to look into the nature of contemporary changes for explanations of witchcraft, aspects such as the decline of the feudal system, religious upheavals, the dispossessions under the Enclosure Laws, the increase in population and a concomitant rise in poverty. In the Pendle Forest, for example, the growing population put considerable pressure on the available land: in 1527 there were a mere 98 tenants of the forest lands, 135 years later the number had more than doubled, to 230. Not surprisingly

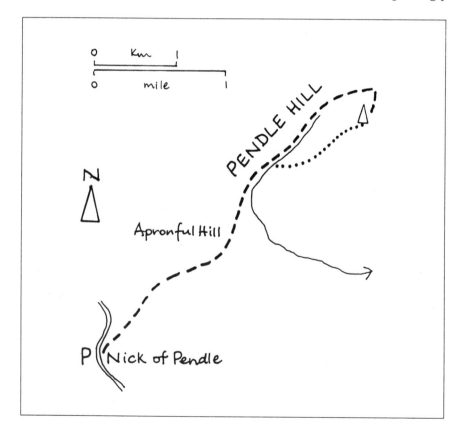

tensions increased which would have adversely affected the climate of social opinion, and no doubt led to all manner of claims and counter-claims.

You begin from the Nick of Pendle, where a broad track sets off north-east across Pendleton Moor and Apronfull Hill. The Nick lies along a road between Sabden to the south and Pendleton to the north. From it the track ambles easily along to Spence Moor before starting to become boggy.

Apronfull Hill is a Bronze Age burial site, but has become renowned in legend as the place from which the Devil bombarded Clitheroe Castle, creating what is today known as the Devil's Window. As you cross to Spence Moor, a valley, Ashdean Clough, appears on the left, while ahead you can see the broad summit of the hill. Soon, still following a clear, if muddy, path, you reach Ogden Clough, a very obvious deep ravine carved over thousands of years by the stream you see down below.

When you reach Ogden Clough the path meets a dilapidated wall, and a short way down in the clough you can see a curving path running with the line of the stream towards the top of the hill. Go down towards this clough path (it is usually drier than staying with the original and higher path) and follow it, ignoring tempting but very boggy direct paths to the summit, until you are virtually thrust into the streambed by a corner of a drystone wall which appears on the left. Keep following the streambed, crossing the stream as necessary, until you finally emerge to follow the line of a wall to the very edge of the eastern escarpment, from where you simply turn right (south) on a broad green path to reach the trig pillar on the summit.

To return either retrace your steps, or head down the boggy path to rejoin the stream in Ogden Clough south-west of the summit, rejoining the outward route there.

Historically, Pendle Hill was one of many beacon hills throughout Britain, and commands a magnificent panorama taking in the industrial townships of Lancashire, the rolling farm fields, the coastline of the Irish Sea and the far fells of Lakeland. Quite splendid!

Walk 25: Spence Moor

Start/Finish: Sabden village car park. GR.779374

Distance: 5 miles (8km)

Height gain: 1015ft (310m)

Walking time: About 3 hours

Type of Walk: A pleasant moorland walk, generally on good paths, farm lanes and tracks.

Maps: All but the first few minutes of the walk is covered by the OS Outdoor Leisure Sheet 21: South Pennines. The missing section will be found on Pathfinder Sheet 680: Longridge and Great Harwood.

Public transport: *Bus:* BPT, LAK, RIB and WLC operate services to Sabden, plus the Pendle Witch Hopper service.

A Taste of Pendle's Moors

The broad grassy expanse of Spence Moor is just one of numerous 'moors' that collectively comprise Pendle Hill, but the only one to enjoy sufficient distinction to stand alone, even though it merges seamlessly with adjoining moors. It lies at the south-western edge of the sprawling Pendle Hill massif, separated from the higher ground of Barley Moor by the deep ravine of Ogden Clough. If approached from the village of Sabden, the open acres of Spence Moor provide an enjoyable short day's outing, especially suitable for winter, when the occasional stretches of boggy ground are reassuringly frozen, and there is less likelihood of disturbing the resident grouse.

Sabden is today renowned for its association with tales of witchcraft, though there is little evidence that Sabden itself was a focus of attention. It is popular, too, for its 'Treacle Mines', a noted and ingenious tourist attraction founded on the much wider-based occurrence in northern England of wells and springs that often con-

Barn ruin, Spence Moor, Pendle

tained curative properties or sticky, 'treacly' substances. During the eighteenth century Sabden was an industrious place figuring largely as a staging post for the many packhorse trains that crossed between the valleys. But its place along an ancient cross-country route pre-dates Norman times.

Begin from the car park at the bottom end of the village, adjoining Sabden Brook, and turn left up the main street to the crossroads. Take the second turning on the right, Wesley Street, and walk up towards the steepled parish church (St Nicholas). On reaching the entrance to the church, go left up the lane to Badger Wells Cottages. Ignore a branching bridleway on your right, this is the way you will return, but continue round bends and up to a junction at Cockshotts Farm. Here go left to cross the stream of Churn Clough, following the lane as it climbs to the right to reach the end of the terraced Badger Wells Cottages.

As you approach the cottages, go to the right of them to access a sunken pathway with a wall on the right, ascending easily to a gate.

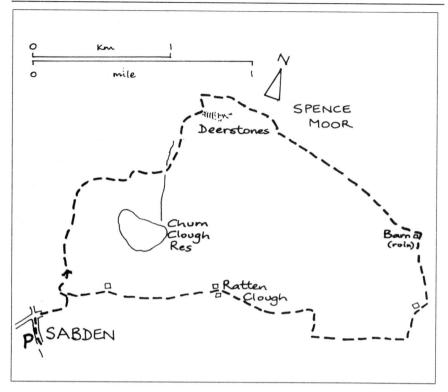

Beyond, a green path trails onwards to another gate, at which you leave the field to pursue a course parallel with Badger Wells Water. Above, on the skyline, the rocky bones of Deerstones poke conspicuously from the landscape like the ribs of a hungry cow.

Continue with the path as it eases upwards, finally reaching the open fellside at a wall and gate. The on-going path rises easily to meet an east-west track. Turn right along it and, by gates, cross the top end of a field before continuing once more above the intake wall.

Through a gap in the wall Churn Clough Reservoir appears below. To complete a very brief stroll you could walk down to the reservoir and then take a stony track out to the access lane serving Ratten Clough Farm, from where you can leisurely return to Sabden.

A short way on the outcrop of Deerstones re-appears. As it does, ignore a branching track on the left, pressing on ahead to descend to cross the tree-lined, stream-filled clough feeding the reservoir. Once across the stream the track rises a little and degenerates into a narrow path as it approaches the perimeter of a larch plantation.

In a retrospective view, the village of Sabden lies cradled in its valley between Black Hill and Wiswell Moor, while to the south rise the twin heights of Great Hameldon and Hameldon Hill, the latter decked with radio masts. Far away to the south-west, Darwen Tower is silhouetted against the skyline, along with more radio masts, this time of Winter Hill, on the edge of the West Pennine Moors.

Follow the boundary of the plantation and descend to cross another stream. Ignore a tempting stile into the plantation, and rise left on a peaty path to begin an assault on the mantle of bracken that cloaks the hillside below Deerstones. At the top edge of the plantation, as it breaks away to the right, keep ahead, rising steadily on a clear path that soon escapes the bracken and peat to pursue a grassy course, gradually approaching and then swinging round above the rocks of Deerstones.

Deerstones was once quarried, as a spread of scattered boulders betrays. Among the boulders are the footprints of a giant, known as 'Owd Nick', who passed this way en route from Hameldon Hill to nearby Apronfull Hill, from where he is said to have thrown a boulder at Clitheroe Castle.

As the path rises above Deerstones, so it meets a prominent path branching left and running across the moor to a stile and wall. Ignore this, and stroll on to the tussocky top of Deerstones before finally crossing to reach the wall and a parallel path. The path leads, right, to a stile, beyond which an initially wet continuation finally moves out on to the higher ground of Spence Moor, bringing into view the rounded dome of Pendle Hill beyond the concealed depths of Ogden Clough. The path does not cross the highest part of Spence Moor, lost amid a thousand tussocks, but continues south-east and descends obliquely to meet a wall at a stile. Along the skyline ahead, Boulsworth Hill dominates, feeding into Black Hameldon and Thieveley Pike beyond the reaches of Burnley.

Across the wall lies the least endearing stretch of the walk, as a path trails down through marshy moorland, an unpleasant but short-lived experience, the worst of which can be avoided. At a gate at the bottom of the hill pasture, the main path branches left, bound for Newchurch-in-Pendle. Ignore this, and keep ahead, descending roughly parallel with a steep-sided ravine to reach the ruins of an old barn, of which only one gable remains standing.

Pass the gable and go through a former gateway, immediately doubling back to the right to reach a dilapidated wall running down to the top edge of the nearby Cock Clough Plantation. Keep to the edge of the plantation, on a descending path, until the wall gives way to a short stretch of wire fence. Here lies a choice of routes. The simplest way on is to keep outside the plantation, descending a sunken pathway to the outskirts of Sabden Fold Farm, and pressing on down, past the farm, to reach a surfaced lane. There, turn right, to go past the farm.

As an alternative, less problematical in very dry conditions or when the water levels are low, you can access Cock Clough at a simple stile just after the wire fence begins. Once in the clough, either try to follow its boundary, or walk away from the fence for a short distance until you are above the stream, and then move left until you can descend a narrow rib to the confluence of two streams. Cross the left-hand stream, and continue moving down through the clough on an indistinct path. Lower down, the wall bends away to the left, and here a broad wedge of ground drops to another confluence of streams, beyond which an improving path goes on down to the bottom of the clough. As you reach the bottom, you need to descend, right, to cross the stream. This might be difficult if there is much water flowing. Once across the stream, the opposite bank is traversed by a precarious and slippery path, before it tackles a brief boggy section to a simple stile over a fence, close by the farm duck pond. Keep ahead to enter a corner of the farmyard at a stile, and walk ahead to reach the surfaced lane, there joining the first of these alternative routes.

Turn right down the lane, and after a short distance go right with it to pass Lower Lane Farm, where the surfaced lane degenerates to a cobbled track flanked by hawthorn and holly, as much of the remaining route will be. During the days when Forest Law prevailed, the hedgerows provided shelter for animals, and the holly winter feed when the surrounding countryside was blanketed under snow.

The track continues to Wood House Farm, immediately fords a shallow stream, and shortly swings right to rise easily to the ruins of Stainscomb, once a fine Tudor farmstead with mullioned windows. As the ruins are reached, the track swings up and left to begin an easy and level promenade bound for the next farm, Ratten Clough. In places the field walls are made of large, up-ended, moss-encrusted flagstones.

Ahead now the steeple of St Nicholas's Church reappears, pinpointing the grey-roofed spread of Sabden, as the farm track eases on pleasantly to Ratten Clough. Go through the farmyard here, making sure to leave all gates as you find them, and then simply follow a surfaced lane, at first across open fields and then once more flanked by thorn and holly to reach New York Farm. From here a narrow lane runs down between hedgerows to rejoin the outward route at Cockshotts Farm. Turn left, and retrace your steps to the car park.

Walk 26: Weets Hill

Start/Finish: Salterforth Wharfe, near Barnoldswick. GR.887454. Free car park

Distance: 9 miles (14.5km)

Height gain: 820ft (250m)

Walking time: 4-5 hours

Type of Walk: Fairly easy: a combination of farm paths, moorland and some easy level walking on a canal towpath.

Map: OS Outdoor Leisure Map 41: Forest of Bowland and Ribblesdale

Public transport: *Bus:* BPT, RIB, PEN and BOR all operate services to Salterforth.

Modest Worthy

In spite of modest height, Weets Hill offers some of the best views in the South Pennines. The walk should be reserved for a good day. Almost half of the walk follows the Pendle Way, a delightful 45 miles (72km) walk of great variety and interest that explores the moorland and rolling hillsides of Pendle witch country.

Set off northwards along the towpath (Leeds and Liverpool Canal) and under the Barnoldswick road, as far as Cockshot Bridge (GR886463). Leave the towpath and turn left over the bridge on to a track across fields. Turn left along a lane to the main road. The continuing path lies 50m/yds to the left, on an unsignposted tarmac drive by a large house, Parklands, then on a rutted track. At the top of the field go through the left of two gates, shortly to reach a farm lane passing Bleak House. Turn right along the lane, then fork left, passing Bancroft Mill.

Turn left into Moorgate Road, to reach Folly Lane which climbs a spur of Weets Hill. Look out for the Pendle Way sign (a witch on a broomstick). It marks a stile in the wall to the right, giving access to a path climbing westwards over high pastures at the spur's edge.

The path becomes a more prominent track and passes through an area once quarried in times past, but now cloaked with grass. Near the top of Weets Hill, a right fork climbs past a stone-built cairn to the summit trig point. The views, always good, have now reached panoramic proportions; Pendle Hill is added to the scene, overwhelming the neighbouring rolling hills.

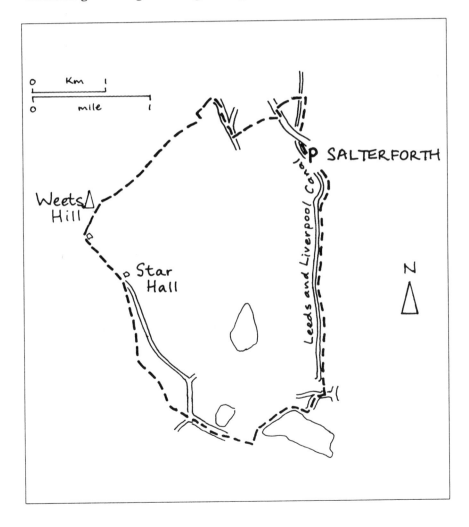

A well-used track heads back to the stone wall. It passes left of Weets House Farm to the end of Gisburn Old Road. Go down past a couple of cottages and Star Hall. Another Pendle Way sign points the way across meadows, heading away from the road by a stone wall.

The path switches to the opposite side of the wall just before reaching a walled track that crosses the route. The Pendle Way proper turns right, into the valley, from here, but maintain direction, following the wall for about 300m/yds. Concealed steps in the wall by a small copse mark the start of the route down to Foulridge. A wall acts as a guide for the first part. When it veers right, keep ahead to the bottom of the field to a stile. Turn right and follow a wall at the top edge of the field. On meeting a path from Malkin Tower Farm, bear left to the bottom of the field. The path goes to the left of a row of cottages to meet a lane.

On the opposite side of the road a path follows the edge of a field and passes between two cottages to reach the road close to the reservoir dam. Turn right along the road to a stony track just beyond the course of an old railway. A waymarked, tree-lined track heads north-east towards Foulridge Lower Reservoir. A path along the northern shores begins from the back of the car park.

After rounding the north-eastern shores go past some houses, and keep north to Sycamore Rise, where you turn right. Turn left on reaching the B-road and follow signs for Foulridge Wharfe, down Warehouse Road, to reach the towpath of the Leeds and Liverpool Canal.

Two miles of towpath lead back to Salterforth Wharfe, a delightfully easy way to end the walk.

Walk 27: Pendle Hill from Downham

Start/Finish: Downham. GR.785442

Distance: 5½ miles (9km)

Height gain: 1395ft (425m)

Walking time: 3-4 hours

Type of Walk: Generally straightforward, but steep both going up and coming down. Wait for a clear day.

Map: OS Outdoor Leisure Map 41: forest of Bowland and Ribblesdale

Public transport: *Bus:* Downham has services operated by LAK, RIB and TCH, as well as the Pendle Witch Hopper Leisure Link during the summer months.

Up Hill and Downham Dale

This is undoubtedly the finest ascent of Pendle Hill, and begins in the delightful village of Downham. Jessica Lofthouse, describing Downham with the eye of one who loves what is old and good, found the village "perfect, with its Anglian village plan facing to street and brook and ring o' roses round the green". Arthur Mee described it as "a bit of Elizabethan England forgotten by time". It boasts a splendid assortment of Tudor, Jacobean and Georgian houses interspersed with weavers' cottages and less noble dwellings built during the eighteenth and nineteenth centuries. Most of the cottages date from these centuries, though there is evidence that there was a Saxon church here during the eighth and ninth centuries. For long the village was closely associated with farming, but has rather relinquished this affinity to cope with the ever-pressing demands of tourism.

The story of Downham is one linked very closely with the Assheton family since the middle of the sixteenth century, when they

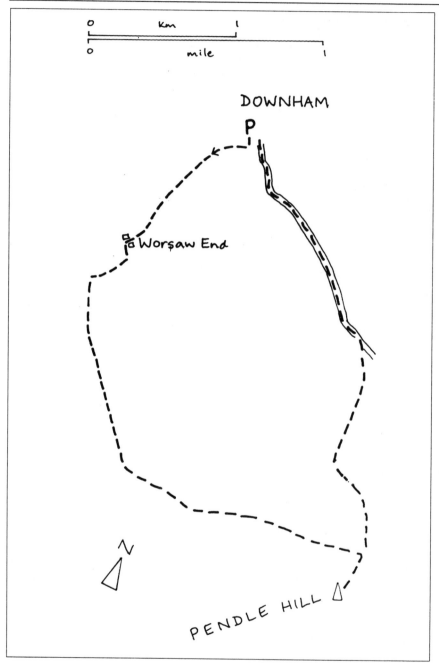

bought the lordship of the manor. It was the diary of Nick Assheton, written in the seventeenth century, which inspired Harrison Ainsworth to pen his evocative tale of the *Lancashire Witches*.

Start from the bridge at the bottom of Downham, turning along a side road to a car park entrance and up a short drive to a couple of houses. Cross a stile by a gate between the houses, and set off beside a fence on the right. When you reach a gate keep on, just outside a wood, and you will emerge into a field. Cross to a fence corner, and on to a corner stile. Cross a field bottom to another stile, then a wall corner, keeping on beside the wall. Just before Worsaw End House, go through a gate and down to join its drive, which leads out on to a lane.

Turn right along the lane and at the second corner, as the road bends right, stick to the 'No Through Road' until it turns sharp left towards a farm, keeping straight on along a green track. At the top a stile puts you on to Pendle's flanks. Go steeply up the right side of a deep ravine until the gradient relents for a while as you haul on to Worston Moor. The path becomes less obvious, but aim for a wall, following this for a while before turning up a sunken way that guides you up more steep ground. With little difficulty you can continue to the prominent landmark of Scout Cairn, from there heading for a stone shelter, beyond which a ladder stile crosses the wall. Now a green track runs on across Downham Moor to another ladder stile from where the summit is only a few minutes away.

To return, go back to the wall, retracing your steps until you can take a narrow path across the moor, heading for Downham. This improves as you descend and meets the track from Barley, but on the way you can take a track (look for a Pendle Way marker), pursuing a steep descent to Fox's Well. Beyond, the path narrows and contours round the northern slopes to join another path that runs clearly down the hillside to reach a stile where the moor is finally left behind. A path leads on through a rough pasture to reach the Pendle road. Turn left down the lane, to reach Downham in about twenty minutes.

Walk 28: Pendle Hill Circuit

Start/Finish: Clitheroe Castle. There is ample parking in the town. GR.743417

Distance: 7 miles (11km)

Height gain: 740ft (225m)

Walking time: 3-4 hours

Type of Walk: A steady up and down walk across the south-western slopes of Pendle Hill.

Map: OS Outdoor Leisure Map 41: Forest of Bowland and Ribblesdale

Public transport: *Rail:* Clitheroe. *Bus:* Numerous bus services operate into Clitheroe, while the Bowland Rambler, Ribble Valley Rambler and Bowland Pathfinder operate during the summer months.

Snapping at the Heels of Pendle

Clitheroe is an attractive, bustling market and former cotton town, the capital of the Ribble valley, lying between the Forest of Bowland and Pendle Hill. It is a small hill town of stone houses gathered around the foremost Norman keep in Lancashire, and marks the northern limit of industrialised Lancashire. It is a town that saw and heard much of the treacherous escapades and dealings of the Norman barons, most of whom spoke no English, conversing in the northern French dialect – an odd thought as you pass through Clitheroe now and listen to the chattering tones of Lancashire and Yorkshire that throng this 'border' town.

The castle used to belong to the de Lacy family, and later, by marriage, to the Earls and Dukes of Lancaster, by which lineage it reached the Crown at the time of Henry IV. What you see of it now is all that remains after Cromwell's order to have it demolished in 1649. In 1660, the castle and the Honor of Clitheroe were given by Charles II to General Monk, who did so much work to bring about the restoration of the monarchy.

But it would not be right to leave Clitheroe without mention of one of the town's much-loved writers, Jessica Lofthouse. A native of Clitheroe, Jessica Lofthouse's study of her native county led to wider exploration, and always with a keen eye for the unusual and with amazing attention to detail. She has long been regarded as a leading authority on the history, folk lore and traditions of Lancashire and the northern countryside generally.

The walk begins from the castle, from where you head down Castle Street, turning right into Wellgate and down Shawbridge, then right and left at the A671 to go along Shawbridge Street. Soon,

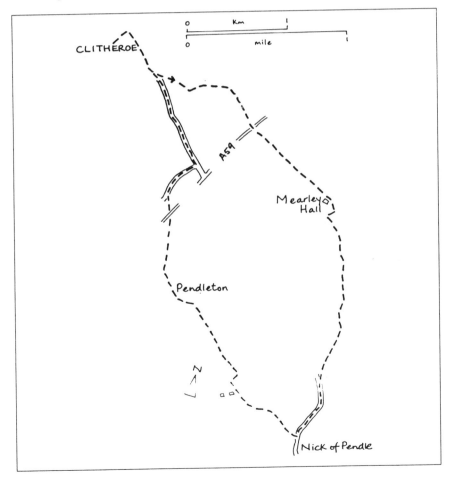

after passing Hayhurst Street, turn left along a track, cross a stream, and stay with the stream. Go through a fence and pass a fairly new housing estate, following a track between hedgerows to a farm. Cross a stile near the farm buildings, and head left along a track at the left-hand edge of a field. When the track heads for another farm, keep ahead along another field margin and follow a succession of stiles until you reach the A59.

Cross the road with care, it is very busy and carries high speed traffic. Over the stile on the far side, keep always ahead, slightly south of east to reach Mearley Hall beneath the soaring slopes of Pendle Hill. Go into the farmyard and keep on to reach a crossroads, there turn right. A short way on turn left at a waymark, climbing through one field and then another to pass a barn. Keep ascending and pass Howcroft Barn and cross Howcroft Brook before rising further to reach the road just below the Wellsprings Inn. From here walk up the road to the Nick of Pendle.

Just below the Nick you gain a slanting pathway (signposted) at a gate on the right. Follow the path down across the hillside to another gate, a few boggy strides beyond which you reach a sunken pathway that runs on down to Wymondhouses Farm.

Go to the right of the farm, cross a couple of stiles, and keep forward along a hedge line. The path now runs on towards the village of Pendleton by sticking to the right-hand edge of a field to another stile where it goes left to reach and cross a footbridge over Swardean Clough. The path continues across more fields, always in a north-westerly direction, until you reach a track that leads you into the attractive village of Pendleton which has a brook running through its centre.

Go through the village and past the Swan with Two Necks, keeping ahead at a signposted path along a track past two houses. Stay close to the hedge on your right, and then go diagonally right across the next field to a stile. Keep on in the same direction until you meet the A59 once more.

Cross the road again, and go down a track opposite to a stile. Go across a field to a stile followed by a footbridge and keep on until you reach a lane. Turn right along the lane to a road junction at Four Lane Ends, and there turn left, following the road back into Clitheroe.

Walk 29: Wiswell Moor

Start/Finish: Spring Wood car park and picnic site. GR.741361

Distance: 6¼ miles (10km)

Height gain: 1035ft (315m)

Walking time: 3-3½ hours

Type of Walk: Interesting circuit of Wiswell Moor, with good views in all directions. Frequently muddy, making stout boots or wellies advisable.

Map: OS Pathfinder Sheet 680: Longridge and Great Harwood

Public transport: *Bus:* LAK run a service to Wiswell.

Wiswell Wander

Extending north-eastwards from Whalley in Calderdale, the wedge of Wiswell Moor is ringed by working farmsteads, many of which give clues to the social history of yesteryear's Lancashire, as well as providing conditions underfoot that call for protective footwear. That minor inconvenience aside, the walk is a pleasant promenade, initially above the Sabden valley, up to the Nick of Pendle, from where it visits a number of interesting farm sites between Pendleton and Wiswell.

Leave the Spring Wood car park and walk out to the main road, turning left to follow a wall for a short distance to a signposted gap giving access to a golf course. Go immediately left, in front of a tee to pass round a large tree on which the letters 'FP' and an arrow have been painted. The on-going path skirts Spring Wood and the edge of the golf course, keeping as much as possible 'out of bounds' until a footbridge is reached beyond the upper boundary of the woodland. Cross the footbridge and head up the ensuing pasture, going between the right-hand two of three oak trees to reach a fence corner. Now follow the fence to the top end of the field, where the fence is crossed by a stile, and two more stiles follow in quick succession.

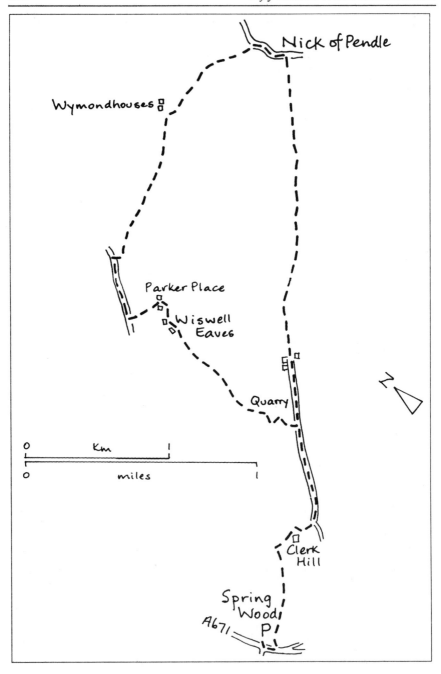

Over the third stile, follow the fence on your left for a short distance, heading roughly for a dilapidated barn, to reach a broad access track. Turn right and use the track to reach the access lane to Clerk Hill at a stone building bearing the initials 'JW' and the date 1772 that now does service as a garage. Clerk Hill is decidedly Georgian in style, its construction having been started by the Whalley family in 1715, during the reign of George I, and completed in 1772, during the reign of George III.

Follow the access road to meet a minor lane, and go left along this to Wiswell Moor Farm, where the surfaced lane degenerates into a broad track. Keep ahead past more farms to lope across the southern flank of Wiswell Moor to Wilkins Hey, and ultimately the Sabden-Pendleton road just below the Nick of Pendle. Sabden shelters greyly in the valley below, while ahead the dark rocky gash of Deerstones and the rounded dome of Spence Moor block views to the north-east. Far away, the massive sprawl of Boulsworth Hill rests on the horizon, while to the south-east radio masts pinpoint Hameldon Hill.

When you reach the road, turn left to go up to the Nick of Pendle, just beyond which you gain a slanting pathway (signposted) at a gate on the left. Follow the path down across the hillside to another gate, a few boggy strides beyond which you reach a sunken pathway that runs on down to Wymondhouses Farm.

The present farm at Wymondhouses dates from the seventeenth century and stands on the site of what was once a small hamlet, first dating from the late thirteenth century. Wymondhouses is also significant as the place where Thomas Jollie (the elder: 1629-1703) was licensed to preach and build meeting-houses following the Revolution in 1688 and the Toleration Act, 1689, which in effect granted freedom of worship to Protestant nonconformists.

Before reaching Wymondhouses, branch left on a poorly signposted, indistinct path that crosses rough ground to the top edge of a field, entering the field by a wooden stile instantly followed by a through-stile. Go left along the top edge of the field to meet and follow Audley Clough, which feeds into the reservoir down to your right. Beyond the reservoir, Longridge Fell and the more distant hills of Bowland dominate the skyline.

Stay with the clough as it shepherds you down to a field corner, where you cross a simple stile, the stream and the clough, on to a rising path into another, large pasture. Head diagonally out across the pasture, targeting Cold Coats Farm. Go through a gate and ahead to another gate beside the farm buildings. Through this you can walk down a short access track to reach a quiet back lane linking Pendleton and Wiswell.

Go left along the lane until, at a footpath signpost, you can turn left to ascend a tarmac lane to Parker Place Farm. Pass between the farm buildings to reach a small wooden gate at the rear of the farmhouse. Turn right, then through a metal gate, and keep ahead across the bottom end of a hill pasture to enter Wiswell Eaves farmyard at a stile beside a gate. Walk on past the farm buildings to locate a gate just to the right of a double garage. Two more gates lead you through an untidy area before you can rise left, slanting across the hillside, eventually to reach another gate where a wall and fenceline meet.

On the skyline to the left a ladder stile beckons, but ignore this, and walk ahead, out across the field to an unseen wall corner where two stiles await, one wooden and the other a gap stile in a wall. Take the gap stile and follow a grassy trod beyond, round a small hillock and down to meet a broad track near the edge of Deer Park Wood. Turn left on to the track, and follow it down, past a quarry, and through a wide stand of gorse, eventually to reach your outward route at a simple stile and five-bar gate near Wiswell Moor Farm, from where you simply retrace your steps to Spring Wood.

Walk 30: Formby and Ainsdale Dunes

Start/Finish: Freshfield Station, between Ainsdale and Formby. GR.291083

Distance: 3½ miles (6km)

Height gain: Virtually none

Walking time: 2½ hours, plus squirrel time

Type of Walk: : Easy and fascinating; a stroll through natural history. Take very warm clothing.

Map: OS Pathfinder 710: Formby and Maghull

Public transport: *Rail:* The walk can be undertaken using Merseyrail's Northern Line, to and from Freshfield Station. Information about rail connections can be obtained from the Merseytravel Line on Tel: 0151 236 7676. *Bus:* Bus services to Freshfield are operated by ABT, CSV and NWR.

Reserved for Squirrels

The name 'Freshfield' has an interesting origin. Between 1750 and 1850 the site of the present village of Freshfield, then called Church Mere, was buried by sand. The area was subsequently made stable by a Mr Fresh, who imported top soil to enable cultivation to take place. As a result the new village was called Freshfield.

This brief walk around Formby Golf Course is especially absorbing during winter, and a perfect break from sitting around the house doing nothing; it makes a pleasant stroll early on a summer's morning, too, when the air is keen and fresh. It visits the coastal sand dunes, where on a windy day you can study the way the sand dunes are formed; almost as primitive and natural a process as the formation of the Antarctic landscape, if you think about it.

In addition, you can visit the National Trust Red Squirrel Reserve, which is open all year, and will prove a source of great delight.

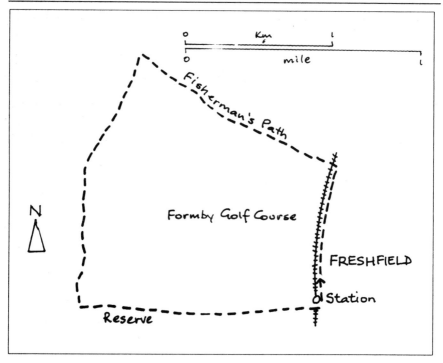

Binoculars are essential if you are to maximise your enjoyment of this walk: seabirds abound at all times of year, and the squirrel reserve is sure to fill more time than you bargained for. The winds that come in from the sea, however, are both strong and cold, and warm clothing is vital during winter months.

The walk begins from Freshfield Station. Walk along nearby Montagu Road, heading northwards, parallel with the railway line, to reach a level crossing, a short distance beyond the end of the houses, across open heathland. You need to cross the railway line, but do so with the utmost care and attention, and do not assume it is safe to cross even when one train has gone by.

On the other side you follow what is known as the Fisherman's Path, which goes ahead through Formby Golf Course, and then through an avenue of pine trees within the Ainsdale National Nature Reserve. The Path is also part of the Sefton Coastal Path. As you approach the shore you are faced with climbing a huge sand dune to reach the beach. Having done so, turn left, at the main junction, along Dune Path South to where it meets the beach. White markers keep you on the correct course since the route is frequently covered with blown sand.

Follow this coastal path through the dunes to Victoria Road, or you can wander along the beach to a path marked "Victoria Road North". Walk up Victoria Road. The National Trust reserve is soon encountered, and really should be visited.

It is a popular misconception that the National Trust manages only stately homes. Far from it. Here you see them working on something that is much different the preservation of red squirrels these are quite tame, and enjoy peanuts. If you want more information about the reserve, ring 01704 878591. The reserve is very well maintained, and has a good network of paths. The office sells nuts, just in case you forget to take some. Your visit, and a small contribution to funds, will be greatly appreciated.

When you have had enough of squirrels, simply continue down Victoria Road, which will soon bring you back to Freshfield Station, and your starting point.

Walk 31: Rufford and Croston

Start/Finish: Croston village. GR.490185. The walk can also be started from Rufford. Parking near the station.

Distance: 12½ miles (20.5km)

Height gain: Virtually none

Walking time: 5 hours

Type of Walk: Very easy tour of Lancashire flatlands along raised embankments and through farm land, but also uses some country lanes. Take care on these. Often wet and muddy, so wellies are advised.

Map: OS Pathfinder Sheet 699: Chorley and Burscough Bridge

Public transport: *Rail:* To Rufford and Croston. *Bus:* Many services link Croston with Southport, Leyland, Preston and Chorley (RIB, NWR, ABT, and FWK).

Twixt Yarrow and Douglas

It was while I was working on one of my walks from Rufford for the Lancashire Evening Post, that I saw the possibility of constructing quite a few routes across the flatlands of the Lancashire Plain from Croston. This is one (or to be exact, two) of them, though judging by the footprints I found, local ramblers and dog walkers know it too, so I claim no originality.

The walk, which is quite long, extends to the village of Mawdesley, but it can be shortened by returning from White Bridge on the edge of Rufford. On a warm summer's day, however, the extended version, perhaps visiting Cedar House Farm, makes a pleasant walk that is nowhere arduous, and makes a grand tour of coastal Lancashire at its best. The drainage needs of such a low-lying area necessarily means that water in one guise or another is never far away. The opportunity should be taken, too, to visit Rufford Old Hall, and doing so will add about half a mile (1km) to the walk.

Croston has quite a history, one of the few really old farming villages of Lancashire, with an interesting fifteenth-century church (St Michael and All Angels) and an old packhorse bridge. To see it now you would not believe that once it was busy with an annual fair and market held under a charter granted by Edward I in 1283, and Feast of St Wilfred, along with weekly markets which drew farmers from far afield. The packhorse bridge, known as Town Bridge, is dated 1682, and has withstood the passage of man and beast, and the floods of the River Yarrow, that it spans, for well over 300 years, and looks good for another three hundred.

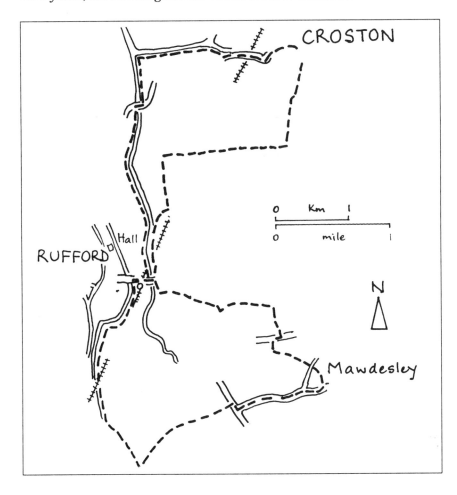

There used to be a village on this site in the seventh century, when the original cross of the Cross Tun or Town was erected by missionaries. The village became the focal point of a massive parish that extended to embrace Chorley and much of the area of Hoole, Hesketh, Tarleton and Bretherton, so large, in fact, that it was divided into four 'quarterings', rather like Melling in Lonsdale.

To begin with, go over the cobbled packhorse bridge spanning the River Yarrow. You'll find it directly opposite the Grapes Hotel. Before you do, notice the blue-faced clock on the church, a tradition of times when gold fingers and numerals on a blue background were considered more legible. Turn left on a surfaced track (Carr Lane) in front of Townbridge Farmhouse and follow it past Manor House Farm for about half a mile. Go right with the track, passing Sumner's Farm and on (Sumner's Lane) to a crossroads near Moss House Farm, and then keep on to reach a railway line. Beyond the level crossing the track continues as High Lane, following an embankment above the surrounding fields that were reclaimed from the bleak mosses of the West Lancashire Plain, probably in the eighteenth or nineteenth century.

At a T-junction, go left on a track by a drainage channel, which after about 600m/yds bends right and left, and then almost immediately right to cross the drainage channel by a footbridge. Now go half left across a field to reach an embankment alongside the River Douglas, climb on to this. Follow the grassy embankment to a white gate at the railway line. Take care crossing the line, and then go down wooden steps to a track. Turn right, and follow the track to a road at White Bridge. If you are returning from this point, or paying a visit to Rufford Old Hall, then turn right, over the bridge.

Otherwise, at the road go left for about 150m/yds and on to a footpath on the left. Go alongside a ditch to the far corner of the field, then right, over a grassy bridge, to reach a farm access. Follow this for half a mile or so to reach New Reed Brook. Leave the access track here and go left along the top of the bank, past a farm bridge, to reach another track, Gales Lane.

Turn right for 100m/yds, then right again over a sleeper bridge, then immediately left, following the field margin to Black Moor

Road. Turn right as far as Sandy Lane, and then left, shortly turning left again to pursue a many-stiled route. This passes an equestrian centre, and keeps ahead across a lane, continuing then to reach School Lane about 400m/yds west of Cedar Farm Galleries and Craft Centre where you can buy refreshments (Open Tuesday to Sunday: 10am – 5pm). You need to turn left on reaching School Lane to get to the farm, and then retrace your steps.

Continue now along School Lane and into Daub Lane to reach Ashcroft's Farm Shop. Turn right, and then left at a footpath sign. Keep close to the field boundary to reach and cross the River Douglas by a footbridge, and then go round a barn to a stile. Waymarks now steer you across the open fields that lie ahead. If you have a dog with you, please keep it on a lead since the fields here are often grazed by sheep, especially during winter.

Eventually, the walk runs out to meet another lane. Turn right as far as the Leeds-Liverpool Canal and Prescott Bridge, and right again along the tow path, following this back to the edge of Rufford.

As you reach the B5246 at or near White Bridge, you can extend the walk to visit Rufford Old Hall, a National Trust property. Whether approaching White Bridge from Croston or Mawdesley, turn into the village (west) to reach the A59, and then turn right and proceed for a short distance to the entrance to the Hall.

Rufford Old Hall is regarded as one of the finest buildings in Lancashire. It is timber-framed in late medieval style and has an impressive Great Hall. It was the home of the Hesketh family for 400 years and was for many years thought to have been started by Sir Thomas Hesketh in 1530, though later research now suggests it was built by Sir Robert Hesketh who was the owner at that time. By the middle of the eighteenth century, manor houses like Rufford were considered unsuited to domestic life, and the family vacated the hall around 1760 when Sir Thomas Hesketh (1727-78) built a more comfortable mansion half a mile away (Rufford New Hall). The Old Hall was, however, reoccupied from around 1825 until it was gifted to the National Trust in 1936. It is a fascinating building and one that will intrigue those with an interest in history.

It is said that William Shakespeare, a long way from home, played here as a young man with Sir Thomas Hesketh's players. The claim is supported if not by direct evidence, then at least by a weight of circumstantial evidence, part of which rests on the terms of the will of Alexander Houghton of Lea Old Hall, near Preston. In it he charged Sir Thomas Hesketh of Rufford to be "ffrendlye unto ffoke gyllome & wllm Shakeshafte nowe dwellynge wth me & ether to take theym unti his Servyce or els to helkpe theym to some good m^{r} [master] as my tryste ys he wyll". The surname 'Shakeshaft' is a common Lancashire variant of Shakespeare, and around this time William Shakespeare, then seventeen, had been sent to work as an assistant teacher to Alexander Houghton's household.

From Rufford return to White Bridge, but do not cross it, instead cross a low stile on the left to gain the western embankment of the Douglas. Now follow this for 1½ miles (2.5km), until you meet the A581 at Great Hanging Bridge.

Note 1: At White Bridge, where the embankment path runs beneath the railway line, the route is often flooded. If this is the case, you should resist the temptation to use the railway bridge to reach the other side, since this would be illegal and potentially dangerous. Instead, walk up the road towards Rufford until you can gain the towpath of the Leeds-Liverpool Canal, and follow that until you meet the A581, which you can then pursue as far as Great Hanging Bridge. Leave the embankment, cross the Great Hanging Bridge, go left over two stiles (waymarked), and back on to the embankment, this time the east bank. Now follow the embankment to where the Douglas and the Yarrow meet, and then turn with the Yarrow and follow its embankment, over stiles, until you come out on the road into Croston. Follow the roads through the village to return to your starting point.

Note 2: The walk as far as White Bridge and back to Croston measures 6½ miles (10.5km), and the Rufford-Mawdesley section a little less. Each half can be done separately if preferred.

Walk 32: The Rainford Loop

Start/Finish: Siding Lane Ranger Centre, Rainford (north-west). GR.465021

Distance: 6 miles (10km)

Height gain: Nominal

Walking time: 3 hours

Type of Walk: Pleasant farm tracks and quiet tarmac lanes make for easy walking.

Maps: OS Pathfinder 711: Wigan and Ormskirk, and 722: St Helens and Huyton-with-Roby

Public transport: *Bus:* ABT, NWR/SLT operate services along the Rainford By-Pass and to Rainford. *Rail:* Rainford (adds about 1 mile each way to the walk).

Winter Wonderland

Although there are a great many footpaths in this southern part of Lancashire (some folk still call it Merseyside, but I learned to drive on the Rainford By-Pass and it was in Lancashire then; to me nothing has changed), you find little effort being put into developing walking routes, though St Helens Countryside Ranger Service and Up Holland Parish Council are notable exceptions.

This tour of the countryside to the west of Rainford is a splendid opportunity to explore the area, and is eminently suitable for the gathering winter months, when warm clothing and a flask of tea or coffee become essential items of equipment. It holds particular appeal for walkers with a keen interest in birdwatching, and begins from the Siding Lane Ranger Centre, north-west of Rainford, and approximately 400m/yds down Siding Lane from the Rainford By-Pass.

Set off west along a tarmac road and at the end go ahead through a stile, keeping a small reservoir to your left. When you reach a large field, take a narrow path (signposted) to the left. A short way on the path widens into a cart track, and about 20m/yds further on, turn left up a small slope to reach the Liverpool to Wigan railway line. You cross the line, but do take great care.

Descend the slope on the other side, and follow a track across fields towards Nursery Plantation. Keep this on your left and continue, to reach a minor lane, Dairy Farm Road. Cross the lane, and follow a signposted path across fields to reach another track.

Keep ahead until shortly after the track bends to the right, you leave it to go left across fields, heading for the buildings at Inglenook Farm, which by now you can see clearly. When you reach another track keep heading towards the farm buildings, but take the first turning on the left to go down to the Rainford By-Pass. When you reach the by-pass, turn right along a cycle lane.

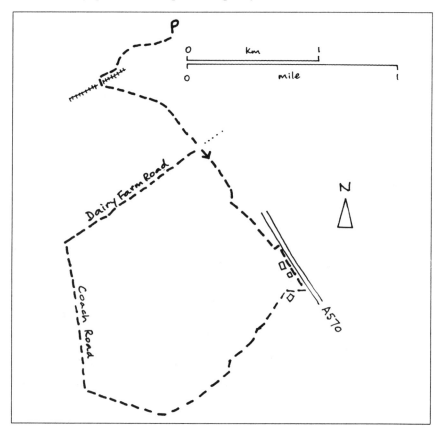

After about 500m/yds of cycle path turn right towards Mossnook Farm, and walk along a track for about half a mile (1km), keeping to the right of the farm buildings, following a hedgerow and passing through two gates. Not long after the second gate you come to another track, and here turn right, soon passing a plantation, Clare's Wood (on your left), to reach a T-junction of tracks. Turn right again. Half a mile (1km) further on, when you reach the old Coach Road to Lord Derby's estate a tree-lined tarmac lane turn right once more, heading north.

This stretch of the walk will particularly interest birdwatchers since the fields frequently host visiting pink-foot geese that arrive in their hundreds from their Arctic summer habitat. Hen harriers, merlin, and other birds of prey also patrol the adjoining fields, and can inject thrilling moments into your day.

I can well recall as a child wondering what or who lay behind the walls of Lord Derby's Estate. That it was Lord Derby was never in doubt, but who he was, what he represented, where he came from, was far too complex a topic to occupy my young mind for longer than the few minutes it would take me to cycle past. Now I know that the family was at the centre of historical action in Britain for over five hundred years. The original family, that of Adam de Aldithlegh, came to Britain with William the Conqueror, and later married a Saxon heiress by the name of Stanley, which name the family adopted in lieu of Aldithlegh.

The Stanleys, as they now were, then went on to acquire a great deal of wealth by judicious marriages, including that of Sir John Stanley who in the fourteenth century married Isabel Latham, heiress to the estates of Knowsley, whose wealth lay in the powerful Hundred of West Derby, from whence ultimately came the new family name. But it was a fifteenth-century descendant, Thomas Stanley, who was made the first Earl of Derby for his action following the Battle of Bosworth Field in placing the crown of England on the head of his stepson, the future Henry VII.

After about three quarters of a mile (1.25km), turn right on to Dairy Farm Road once more, and keep going until you return to the spot where you crossed the road earlier in the walk. Now simply retrace your steps to the ranger centre.

Walk 33: Ashurst Beacon and Beacon Country Park

Start/Finish: Visitor Centre, Beacon Country Park. GR.505066

Distance: 3 miles (5km)

Height gain: Nominal

Walking time: 2 hours

Type of Walk: Very easy walking on good paths. Harts Lane can be slippery at times.

Map: OS Pathfinder 711: Wigan and Ormskirk (Note: The Country Park's own map is to a larger scale.)

Public transport: Many bus services linking Skelmersdale and Wigan pass through Hall Green; this walk can then be started at Hart's Lane car park.

Beacon View

Located on the west-facing slopes of Ashurst Beacon, and so lying to the east of the sprawling mass of the Skelmersdale agglomeration, Beacon Country Park is the principal countryside facility owned and managed by West Lancashire District Council. It is an area of gently rolling fields, woodland, ponds and wide-ranging views, and eminently suited to free-range walking along its vast network of pathways. Canine companions will find it a wonderful place, too.

At its simplest you don't need a walk to follow, you can simply plug into the park from a number of centres Up Holland, Tanhouse, Elmers Green and Dalton, and spend an enjoyable day wandering about its welcoming area. A visitor centre, with café and bar, adjoining a golf course and driving range, means that you can get a cup of tea and a bite to eat. But check the times of opening first by telephoning 01695 622794.

This brief and gentle walk makes a tour of the park and visits Ashurst

Wood carving, Beacon Country Park

Beacon. What it lacks in length it makes up for in quality, and you soon discover what a classic vantage point the high ground of the country park proves to be, from which the greater part of coastal Lancashire and much of Lancashire-turned-Merseyside rolls away in a seemingly endless flow of greenness. The brief extension to visit Ashurst Beacon, a most prominent Lancashire landmark, can be tackled at either end of the walk, and the whole experience rounded off in the visitor centre.

Begin from the visitor centre car park, and go across the car park to its far left corner. There follow a path across a field, keeping your eyes open for some wood carvings that lurk among the trees. Go left, along a woodland edge, and then right, now following the top edge of the wood, to a junction. Go right, and soon, left, on a grassy path with more woodland on your left. A short way on, Carr Lane Car Park appears up on your left, with a pond and footbridge just in front of you. Keep all these to your left, and walk ahead on a broad green path across a field, heading for Harts Lane Car Park, which you can now see directly ahead.

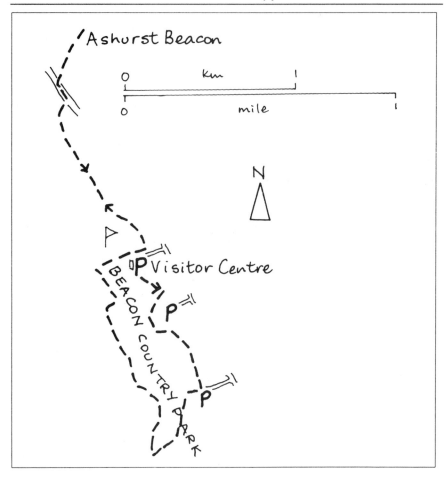

From the car park, which lies about half a mile along Mill Lane from the nearest public transport stop at Up Holland, walk to a wall gap stile, beside an interesting old plough ('The Dandy'), and immediately set off along hedgerow-flanked Hart Lane. The old surface of the lane, which must have witnessed the tread of countless feet over the centuries, pokes through fallen leaves and twiggy debris, here cobbled, there tarmacked, and can be a little slippery underfoot. Keep following this gradually descending lane, with interesting glimpses through the hedges, and occasional wide-open fields for doggy exercise, if necessary.

After about 600m/yds, at an obvious junction (though there are earlier ones, to be ignored), you leave the lane, going right, through an adjoining hedgerow, and rising a little on a grassy path. In strides, sadly, you are within sight and the invasive sound of the A577, Stannanought Road, but head steadily away from it to pass through a hedgerow ahead, with a small pond just off to its right. Keep ahead here, pressing on across another meadow, and through another hedge gap to a crosspath junction. Always keep ahead, and as the path goes on, so the view southwards across the Lancashire Plain to the grey spread of Liverpool and the distant heights of North Wales gradually opens up. A broad sweep right, followed by a sharp left through a hedge gap, brings you out to Elmers Green Lane. Turn right, and walk up between a golf driving range (right) and the Beacon Golf Course, to reach the visitor centre car park. You can end the walk at this point, or go left on a footpath that leads round The Beeches to join Beacon Lane not far from a prominent track that takes you up to the Ashurst Beacon picnic site.

As a viewpoint, Ashurst Beacon has been popular for centuries, indeed, in the 1760s it was described as "the pleasantest place, the most gallant prospect", a place from which it was boasted you could see sixteen counties. In medieval times the coastal lands of Lancashire that you can see from Ashurst Beacon formed part of the West Derby Hundred, held by Edward the Confessor (1042-66). Much of the landscape comprised peatmoss and woodland. Even here, in the most cultivated of Hundreds, there was as much woodland as arable land, while the peatmosses accounted for almost five times the area of land covered by arable and wooded land combined. Ashurst Beacon, which lies along an upland ridge, would have been extensively wooded, and would have provided valuable food, in the form of acorns and beechmast, for pigs.

It is all so different now, though it would always have taken an exceptionally clear day, good eyesight, and a quantum leap of faith to identify sixteen counties.

Walk 34: Cuerden Valley and the River Lostock

Start/Finish: Car park, Sheep Hill Lane. GR.569229

Distance: 5½ miles (9km)

Height gain: Nominal

Walking time: 3 hours, or as long as you want

Type of Walk: Easy rambling around country pathways and through the Cuerden Valley Park.

Map: OS Pathfinder 688: Preston (South) and Leyland

Public transport: *Bus:* RIB operate services along the A6, which is just over half a mile (1km) from the start of the walk.

River Valley Ramble

The delightful Cuerden Valley Park on the northern edge of Chorley is managed by the Lancashire Wildlife Trust, and visitors will find it a splendid place to visit, especially coming into spring, when the trees are alive with birdsong, and the new season's hungry offspring are imposing their tiresome burden on their parents.

The park forms part of the Cuerden Estate, through which runs the River Lostock. Many parts of the park are still actively farmed, and there is a good diversity of flora and fauna. The park includes examples of Iron Age hilltop settlements, medieval water-meadow leats and early field boundaries, though none is especially discernible by the untrained eye. Cormorants, herons, tufted ducks, great crested grebes and Canada geese make full use of a pond in the park, while kingfishers, sand martins and buntings patrol the banks of the River Lostock. Up above in the woods, many warblers appear, to swell the resident population of great, coal, blue and long-tailed tit, nuthatches, green and greater spotted woodpecker, jays, goldfinches, greenfinches, siskin and redpoll. In spring and summer,

The face in the tree, Cuerden Valley Park

peacock, small blue, meadow brown, wall brown and small heath butterflies populate the park, and help to make this a perfect place to wile away a few hours. The walk that follows is one of my favourites, and begins from a car park just off the B5256, at the bottom of Sheep Hill Brow. The first stage of the walk is a loop, reaching as far as Whittle-le-Woods, before returning to the B5256. If you wish, you can split this walk into two shorter walks.

Leave the car park and turn right. Walk along the road for a short distance until, after having crossed Clayton Bridge, you can go left through a gate on to a gravelled path, flanked by scrubby trees. Another gate gives access to a path running along below a field belonging to Clayton Hall Sand Company. At a third gate the path opens out into a broader track through more open woodland, as it runs down to join the River Lostock.

When the path forks, branch right. After a while, as you pass more sand quarry workings and an old pond overgrown with bulrushes, the church of St John the Evangelist at Whittle-le-Woods comes into view.

The track runs out to another car park, but go through a gate and

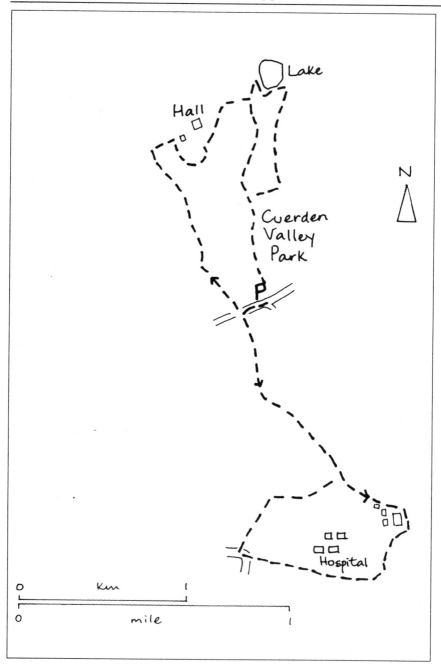

Lake

Hall

N

Cuerden
Valley
Park

P

Hospital

0   Km   1

0   mile   1

keep ahead on to a surfaced lane that leads past Rose Cottage and the rear of a factory unit to a footpath sign on the right. Leave the lane for the footpath, which leads to the edge of a cricket field. Keep to the right-hand edge of the field to an open gate at another lane. [If you feel concerned about walking around the edge of the cricket field when there is a match in progress, you should backtrack until you are between the factory building and Rose Cottage, and there turn left on a lane that leads past cottages to a bridge. There rejoin the original line and turn right (before the bridge), over a stone stile to continue beside a stream as follows.]

Turn right on the lane, over a bridge, and immediately left over a stone stile on to an overgrown path running beside a stream. The path continues to a couple of low metal stiles (one with a dog gate), and continues along the bottom edge of a pasture from which it is separated by a barbed wire fence. Beyond another stile the path continues in much the same direction, and runs on into a green lane flanked by beautiful beech trees leading up to hospital grounds.

Keep ahead on a surfaced lane at a crossroads at the entrance to the hospital grounds until you emerge on to Dawson Lane. A short way on turn right, taking the access road to the sand quarry. Follow the access as far as a footpath sign on the right, and there turn right, over a stile (dog gate) to re-enter the grounds of the Cuerden Valley Park. The on-going path runs along the edge of a meadow, rising slightly before descending to another gate near a pond, and a path that runs out to rejoin your outward route near the River Lostock. Now turn left and retrace your steps, remembering, when the path forks, to branch left and so gain the path that will lead you back to Clayton Bridge.

As you emerge on the B5256 once more, turn left for a short distance to a footpath sign on the right. Cross a stile, and then ascend obliquely left, eventually to reach another stile at Sandy Lane. Turn right along the lane, taking care against traffic, until you reach the entrance to Cuerden Hall and the offices of the Lancashire Wildlife Trust. Follow this access, bearing right when it does, and soon branch right, through a gate, to see a face carved in a tree, one of a number of tree carvings in the vicinity which, so I'm told, were done by a man from Bretherton, though no one seems able to tell me more.

Walk past the face carving, following a path that circles left and eventually rises to meet a broad track at a gate close by the offices of the Wildlife Trust – why not bob in and join, if you are not already a member, or buy a copy of their excellent magazine *Lapwing*?

Turn right on the track, and follow this past distant Cuerden Hall. There has been a house here since 1717. Later, Mr Robert Townley commissioned Lewis Wyatt to design a new mansion (1816-19), and it was during this period that the formal landscapes and ornamental lake of present-day Cuerden Valley Park were laid out. The hall was acquired by the Tatton family in 1906, and during World War I was used as a military hospital. In 1939, the hall was requisitioned as an army education centre and later as the headquarters of an anti-air-craft command. The estate was auctioned off to private landowners for agricultural use in 1954, and in 1958 the hall was purchased by the Ministry of Defence and became the regional army headquarters. In 1977, the hall and estate were compulsorily acquired by the Central Lancashire Development Corporation, and a proposal put forward to develop the estate as a valley park for informal recreation. The hall is now used as a nursing home by the Sue Ryder Foundation.

Having passed Cuerden Hall, the path descends, right, to cross the River Lostock at a stone, arched bridge. Over the bridge you have a choice. The quickest way back to the start is to turn right on a broad track that will lead you directly back to the car park in about twenty minutes. Or, ignore this and go half-left across a grassy area to a flight of wooden steps. At the top of these you emerge on the edge of a pond which is host to a surprisingly wide range of birds. Walk around the pond until your path joins another and you face a gate a short way ahead. Walk towards the gate, and then branch right, climbing a little into woodland that in spring is carpeted with bluebells, and in winter shelters many more birds including siskin, redpoll, green and great-spotted woodpeckers.

Follow the undulating path through the woodland until, near another gate, you can branch right, down more steps, and follow a descending path beside a stream to the main valley path. When you do, go left, and follow the broad track out to reach the car park from where the walk began.

Walk 35: Wigan Pier to Haigh Country Park

Start/Finish: Wigan Pier. GR.579051

Distance: 5½ miles (9km) [or 9 miles (15km)]

Height gain: 400ft (120m)

Walking time: 2-3 hours

Type of Walk: Easy, on towpaths and roads. Keep dogs on leads and children under control on and while crossing the roads, all of which are busy.

Map: OS Pathfinder 711: Wigan and Ormskirk, and 712: Bolton (South)

Public transport: *Bus:* A number of operators run services to Wigan (RIB, NWR and GMB). *Rail:* Wigan is on the main west coast line, and is reached by cross-country services from Manchester, Liverpool, Preston and the coast.

The Way We Were

If I were to say harsh things of Wigan, a place where I lived and worked for more than sixteen consecutive years (21 in total), the town, even assuming it noticed my outburst, would just shrug and carry on. Such indifference to adverse comment has been a feature of Wigan for many years. Arthur Mee, writing about Lancashire says: "Who has not said hard things of it, not knowing it? It is a wilderness of dullness, we are told, a place of slums whose people live their dreary round in dark and tasteless streets, with nothing beautiful to see." Pevsner said, "Wigan has been much maligned as the *nec plus ultra* of Lancashire gloom."

Well, at least I know Wigan, and I can assure you that the opinions expressed by Mee and Pevsner (not their own, I hasten to add) are now a long way from the truth. How successful the change has been is too subjective an opinion to matter, but, thankfully, the town

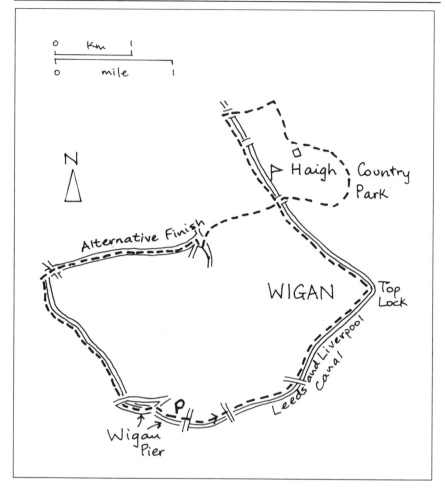

makes what it can of its heritage, and could make more if the exact site of the Roman settlement of Coccium was known for certain. And if the town centre buildings do echo some of the best examples of the worst kind of modern architectural design, at least when you visit Wigan Pier, travel its waterways, or visit the estate of the Earls of Crawford, you become aware that here is a town that cares about its past, and has much to care about. This walk takes the opportunity to do all these things, and takes you from the centre of town out into beautiful countryside (perhaps not as much appreciated by the town fathers as it should be).

The walk begins from the Mill at the Pier car park, which is convenient for the café on site when you return, though you will find another at the half-way stage, if you prefer. The route is given in two parts. The first goes up to Haigh Country Park and then returns by the same route. The second turns the walk into a circular tour, returning to the Pier along the westerly section of the Leeds and Liverpool Canal. This unfortunately involves a mile or so of walking through a busy and uninspiring residential area to rejoin the canal, but the choice is yours.

As a pier, of course, Wigan Pier never existed, being no more than the product of a waggish wit that on a return train journey from a holiday to Blackpool and its seaside piers responded to being asked where they were by joking, "We're at Wigan Pier." George Formby, that loveable Lancashire comedian, immortalised Wigan Pier in one of his songs, while the heavier and more serious pen of George Orwell (after whom a pub is now named) covered a wider ranges of issues in his book *The Road to Wigan Pier*, a documentary account of working class life in the North of England in the 1930s. Orwell (real name Eric Blair) visited Wigan for a few days in 1936.

Today what you find is a complex of old canalside warehouses converted into a series of exhibitions and museums under the banner 'The Way We Were'. There was even a time when the modern 'pier' enjoyed its own Piermaster, but such sound promotional imagery is sadly a thing of the past.

So, to the walk. From the car park go out to reach the towpath of the Leeds and Liverpool Canal, passing first beside the barge 'Roland' and into a small garden area. Turn left on the towpath, and walk away from the pier complex, soon crossing Poolstock Lane (with care, because you do so on a bad bend), and then quickly resume the towpath, heading for Ince.

You cross the A577 road to Hindley at Rose Bridge. Beyond, you almost immediately encounter the first of the locks that lead, it won't surprise you to learn, to Top Lock. If you choose a summer weekend to do the walk the chances are that the locks will be constantly in use, and you can pass a few idle moments figuring out the sequences that have to be followed to raise or lower canal barges through this complex system.

At Top Lock turn left on the towpath, which shortly passes

beneath the road to Aspull, and continues to reach the boundary of Haigh Country Park. As you reach the bridge that carries the main driveway up to Haigh Hall (if you reach the golf course on the right you have gone too far), leave the towpath on the left and ascend to the driveway.

Turn right and across the canal, and a short way on branch left, off the main drive, to follow a rough track through woodland. You are now in Haigh Country Park, one of the first in England to be so designated, and fashioned about the former estate of the Earls of Crawford. Its mix of woodland and habitat shelter a wealth of flora and fauna.

When the main drive is encountered again further on, cross it, and continue on a rough track. In due course, you cross the line of the miniature railway that operates as a leisure attraction during the summer months. Keep ahead, passing the Swan Pond, and eventually the track brings you out near a children's play area adjoining the Stables block, which now houses a small café and information centre/gift shop. Haigh Hall is just off to your left, and to reach it you need to branch left as you reach the children's play area.

In the twelfth century the manor of Haigh was held by a Norman, Hugh le Norreys, and by 1295 it was the property of Mabel, who was married to Sir William Bradshaigh. The Hall is the second to be built on this site, being constructed during the reign of George IV by James, who became the 24th Earl of Crawford in 1825 and was made Baron Wigan of Haigh Hall. Work began on the Hall in 1827 and was finished around 1840 (though some sources say 1849). The old hall had been significantly enlarged during the reign of Elizabeth I, but was later much neglected. It was to Earl James that the task of rebuilding fell. Fortunately, he was an engineer, and drew his own plans, directed the building operations himself, and used his own materials. While work was proceeding he lived in one of the cottages on the estate, and earned for himself the nickname "Jimmy in the Trees".

His successor, the 25th Earl of Crawford, who was an accomplished scholar and traveller, amassed a library of great value, thought to have been the best private library in the country, much of which was transferred to the John Rylands Library in Manchester. The library contained over 5 000 oriental and ancient European manuscripts dating from the sixth century, many written on tree bark, papyrus and vellum.

The Hall is not open to the public, though it is used for banqueting and conference purposes, and even as I write, the future of the Hall is the subject of debate, for the fourth time to my knowledge.

Having visited the Hall, go round the building and continue ahead, passing the Stables block, to reach and cross the car park. As you leave the car park, turn left on a narrow lane, taking great care against approaching traffic since there is no footpath here. Continue as far as the second turning on your left, Pendlebury Lane, and go down this to reach the canal. Just over the canal bridge you can descend left (slippery when wet) to reach the towpath, and can now follow this pleasantly back to the bridge bearing the main drive.

From this point you can either go under the bridge and return to Wigan Pier along your outward route, or you can turn right down the main drive for a short distance until you can branch right into Hall Lane. Here you pass a couple of renovated cottages on the right which once housed estate workers. Keep ahead down Hall Lane, which is flanked by meadows and cottages, to a sharp double bend where the road negotiates the River Douglas. Stay on the rising lane and walk up to the A49, reaching it not far from Wigan Infirmary.

Cross the A49, and go right to the Cherry Gardens roundabout. Turn left and then branch immediately right to head down towards Beech Hill. A little over a mile of road walking now takes you through Beech Hill to cross Woodhouse Lane (busy crossroads/traffic lights), continuing ahead for a few hundred metres until you can leave the road and drop left on to the canal towpath. Now follow the towpath all the way back to Wigan Pier, noting, where the canal dog-legs right, the change line (or changeling) bridge that enabled horses towing barges to change from one side of the canal to the other without uncoupling the towrope where it was necessary to change the towpath from one side of a canal to the other. These were also known as crossover, turnover, roving and snake bridges, though strictly speaking the term 'roving' should only be applied to a bridge that was built at a junction of canals, not as here at Wigan, where the canal simply changes direction.

Walk 36: Around Pennington Flash

Start/Finish: Car park, pay and display, Pennington Flash. GR.643991.

Distance: 3 miles (5km)

Height gain: None worth talking about

Walking time: 1½-2 hours

Type of Walk: Delightful waterside ramble. Binoculars essential. Wonderful for dogs, but they must be kept under control.

Map: OS Pathfinder Sheet 723: Eccles

Public transport: *Bus:* Numerous bus services operate out of Leigh, passing the entrance to Pennington Flash Country Park.

Leigh Flash

In the days before local government reorganisation in 1974, Leigh Borough Council worked hard in a corporate venture with Atherton and Tyldesley Urban District Councils to develop the opportunities for sport and recreation in their areas. Leigh's task, I was then its Deputy Town Clerk, was to improve the area around Pennington Flash, to do something about the unsightly colliery spoil heaps that flowed from Bickershaw Colliery, and to build a golf course. It was no easy task because much of the land around the flash was prone to flooding from time to time, and I still remember pictures of railway engines ploughing through shallow lakes that overflowed on to the railway lines.

Much of the ultimate responsibility for developing the flash into its present status as a major ornithological site in Britain fell to the new Council in Wigan, and in the late 1980s I resumed my responsibility for overall management of the site. The site is especially noted for its birdlife, having been visited by a number of rarities and the associated gaggle of 'twitchers'. I recall that on one day a few years ago I saw a little ringed plover, spoonbill, wood sandpiper and short-eared owl, all then new additions to my list of British birds.

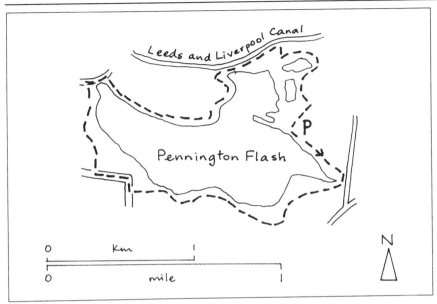

Twenty years ago it was only with great difficulty that you could walk around the Flash; now all you need is a pair of wellies. I say wellies because some stretches are over cloying mud, though the worst of it can be avoided.

You start from the car park near the golf club house, where numerous black-headed gulls, ducks, geese, swans, and even the odd redshank try to pick a living. You'll have to pay for parking, unless you use one of the lay-bys along the access road. Because the walk never moves far from a large expanse of water, the air temperature experienced on the walk can often be quite cold, so wear something warm, and do remember to take binoculars.

Leave the car park, heading away from the buildings along a constructed path beside a car park extension. Cross a wooden footbridge and turn right on to a track running round the narrow outlet from the Flash. When, almost immediately, the track forks, branch left, and then again, in a few strides, branch right along a track signposted as a Pony Trail.

The trail runs on, never far from the water's edge, through willow scrub, hawthorn and bramble. When, further on, the path forks again, branch right on a track signposted to Green Lane. Keep left when it branches down to the lakeshore, and further on, when the path forks yet again, branch right between wire fences to reach an open pasture, with the lake just on your right.

Follow the path round to the left, on a broad track. When the track reaches a T-junction, opposite a low bench, turn right, heading towards a group of buildings. The path continues between fences, and crossing stiles, at the rear of an industrial area. This brings you out to the buildings. Keep them on your left, and go ahead, through a gate, on to Green Lane, a broad track that runs out, becoming better surfaced, to pass the entrance to sailing clubs.

Keep on to the end of the road, and turn right, following the road round a bend, and on for a further 250 m/yds or so to a signposted footpath on the right. Go down the access road to Mossley Hall, passing in front of the buildings, and going right over a stile on to a wooded path to another stile, beyond which the path skirts a field boundary. Follow this round the far end of the Flash, cross a concrete bridge, and walk on towards the road ahead. As you approach the road, branch right on a path that leads you to a parking area not far from colliery spoil heaps.

This next section is rather claggy underfoot, so if you want to avoid it you can walk up the road as far as the canal, and turn right on to the towpath.

Slant right across the parking area, and walk ahead, crossing the flank of the spoil heaps on your left, and with the edge of the flash on your right. Press on, following the edge of the flash, invariably with a delightful range of wildfowl bobbing about on the water for company coot, cormorant, tufted duck, mallard and wigeon, for example.

Keep following the water's edge around a broad headland until you can go right, through sparse woodland, and eventually meet a broad, muddy track below the canal embankment. If conditions underfoot are especially muddy, go up on to the canal towpath. Either way, keep going as far as a constructed path near a canal bridge.

Turn right at this point, and then immediately left, on another gravel path that, if you stick with it, will lead you all the way back to the car park, passing a few bird observation hides on the way.

Walk 37: The Bold Loop

Start/Finish: St Helens Junction railway station. GR.536933

Distance: 9 miles (14km)

Height gain: Nominal

Walking time: 3½-4 hours

Type of Walk: Easy. Further information is available from the St Helens Countryside Ranger Service (Tel: 01744 739252).

Map: OS Landranger 108: Liverpool and surrounding area

Public transport: *Rail:* Rail Service to St Helens Junction. *Bus:* MPT and GMB operate services to Sutton, where this walk starts.

Taking a Bold Line

It is amazing the amount of confusion that can be caused by local government boundary changes. This walk begins in Sutton, a suburb of St Helens, my home town, and since 1974 part of the Merseyside Metropolitan County. Now the county has gone, and a unitary authority, ironically not much different in powers from the county borough council that first gave me work in 1960, has appeared in its place. As far as I am concerned, this is and always will be Lancashire.

This moderate walk concentrates on an area that has great historical significance both to St Helens and the former county of Lancashire, being based on the stronghold of the Bold family, whose presence in the area pre-dates Edward the Confessor (1042-66). You begin from the St Helens Junction railway station, heading down Station Road to a T-junction. Go right, beneath the railway bridge, and continue as far as Bold Road, the next major junction ahead. Turn left, and after about 300m/yds turn on to a footpath on the right, setting off across fields, with a ditch on your left.

In time, you cross the ditch by a footbridge, and move along to

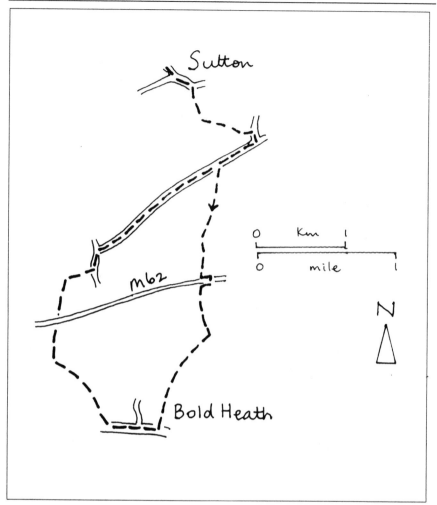

another footbridge. Cross and press on to reach a bungalow. Turn right, then left into Rosehill Avenue, keeping on for a short distance until you can turn right into Neills Road and continue to Gorsey Lane. Cross the lane and go right.

After about 400m/yds, turn left near Park Cottage, go down Hall Lane, and keep going for about half a mile, where you can bear left on a signposted footpath. The path takes you out over fields towards the power station at Fiddlers Ferry, then crosses the M62 motorway by a footbridge, a wonderful place to contrast your leisurely amble and the frenetic and noisy activity below.

Once beyond the motorway, follow the ensuing path round to your right and cross a stile. Soon the path bends to the left and heads towards Old Bold Hall Farm, set neatly amid woodland. This is the site of the former Manor House of the Bold family. Bold Hall has been pulled down, but it dated from around 1732.

On reaching the woodland, follow the path, and go between gateposts, and across a moat bridge, keeping the buildings to your right. The on-going track now runs on for three quarters of a mile to reach Warrington Road, on the outskirts of Bold Heath. Turn right, soon to cross Clock Face Road and School Lane. Then turn right, just after Holly House, on to a tarmac track (signposted). Near the site of Nursery Farm go over a stile and continue up the left side of a field to cross a footbridge, and press on, now along the right side of a field. When the path bears left towards Tibb's Cross Farm, keep to the right of a hawthorn hedgerow. At the farm, turn left, and immediately right, keeping to the left of the house.

The path goes on towards an old railway line (St Helens and Runcorn), but just before the line, turn right, and keep to the left edge of the field, without crossing the nearby fence. Eventually you walk up a small slope, and over a stile, carrying on up the left side of the field to a fence and a line of bushes. Bear right and go over a fence stile. Turn left, and keep to the edge of the field until you are once more parallel with the old railway.

At Union Bank Lane, turn left over a bridge, and then right. Follow the path beneath the M62 (use a fenced concrete walkway), to continue heading northwards along the left side of the old railway line. Four hundred m/yds further on, cross the trackbed and walk to the right of railings to reach Clock Face Road. Cross the road and turn left, towards Clock Face. Turn right on to Gorsey Lane after about 250m/yds, and follow the lane for half a mile before taking to a footpath, after a group of buildings. Then take the first path you encounter on your right and follow this to one of the footbridges you crossed earlier in the walk, from where you simply retrace your steps to the station.

Walk 38: Boulsworth Hill

Start/Finish: Car park on the Trawden-Wycoller lane. GR.926395

Distance: 8 miles (13km)

Height gain: 1115ft (340m)

Walking time: 5 hours

Type of Walk: A moderate circular walk on farm lanes, with a stiff climb over rough, wet moorland.

Map: OS Outdoor Leisure Map 21: South Pennines

Public transport: *Bus:* There is no direct service to Wycoller. BPT/KDT and ELM operate services along the A6068 to Colne and to Trawden.

Brontë Inspiration

Boulsworth Hill at 1695ft/517m is the highest peak in a vast wedge of moorland between the Calder valley at Todmorden and the Aire valley at Keighley. Much of the hill is prohibited to walkers, conceivably a reminder of the days in 1942 when a massive area was destroyed by fire, though it also 'enjoys' the other extreme, as in May 1989 when it experienced a thunderstorm of millennial proportions.

This walk, however, explores an interesting approach from Wycoller, a pleasant village with Brontë associations, for it was to Wycoller that Charlotte Brontë came across the moors from her home in Haworth and saw the ruins of Wycoller Hall. This was once the home of the Hartleys and the Cunliffes, built at the end of the sixteenth century but deserted in 1818. From this visit Charlotte transformed the imagery into Ferndean Hall of *Jane Eyre*.

The route involves tackling steep northern slopes, but rewards you with a breathtaking view across the towns of East Lancashire to the hills and mountains of Bowland, Pendle and the Yorkshire Dales. Much of the land around Wycoller now forms part of a country park, and is still extensively farmed.

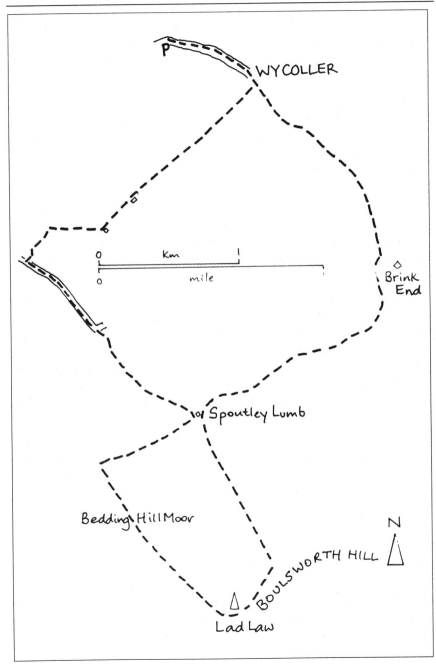

Start from the car park on the Trawden – Wycoller lane which dips into Wycoller village and transports you into a 17th-century scene, where picturesque weavers' cottages huddle together in a narrow verdant vale. The lane follows Wycoller Beck south-eastwards through a tree-lined dean.

Soon, abandon the lane for a track across the beck towards Dean House Farm. The route, signposted initially to Trawden, begins from a stile and then romps across a small field to cross Turnhole Clough, a tributary of Wycoller Beck, by a footbridge. The way then goes left along the upper banks of a wooded glen, entering the woodland for a short time before continuing across wild, bracken-clad fellsides.

The path descends to the stream before climbing to join a track from Brinks End. This old packhorse route soon courses south-westwards, becoming intermittently paved with weather-beaten slabs of millstone grit.

The ascent of Boulsworth Hill, a North West Water courtesy route, begins by the lonely farm of Spoutley Lumb, on a concrete road that climbs south-eastwards to a small reservoir. From here, a way-marked path rises steeply on to Pot Brinks Moor, reaching the ridge at a few small gritstone outcrops known as The Little Chair Stones. The ensuing route across the wide, peaty ridge climbs easily to the Weather Stones, a collection of eroded crags that offer shelter and a good lunch spot.

Boulsworth Hill's summit, Lad Law, lies a little to the west, marked by a trig point set close to gritstone crags, and gives striking views over the industrial towns of Colne, Nelson and Burnley to Pendle Hill and further afield.

The way back starts by a well-defined path across Bedding Hill Moor, returning to the track used earlier, but a little further to the west. This time turn right and follow the track back to Spoutley Lumb Farm. Cross the ladder stile at the far end of the farm and follow a wall on the left. When the wall ends keep on in the same direction through a grassy hollow to reach a bridge over a stream. A short detour to the left leads to Lumb Spout, a pleasant waterfall cascading over a sandstone cliff in a sylvan hollow of oak, ash and rowan.

Return to the bridge, where the walk continues across fields, passing to the right of a farm (Lodge Moss) before meeting a narrow country lane. Follow this downhill to a large mill at Hollin Hall, south of Trawden.

Take the track (signposted to Wycoller and Raven's Rock) at the far end of the mill. It crosses pastures and bends acutely left towards Far Wanless Farm. Leave it here and climb a sad stile for a path bearing half right by a wall. After Little Laithe Farm the way continues north-eastwards by the wall, to the left of Germany Farm and Raven's Rock Farm, crossing several primitive stiles and a couple of dykes. Beyond Raven's Rock Farm the path drops through a plantation of larch, birch, rowan and alder to reach a stony track which takes you back into Wycoller village.

Walk 39: Black Hameldon

Start/Finish: Worsthorne village. GR876325

Distance: 8½ miles (14km)

Height gain: 885ft (270m)

Walking time: 3-3½ hours

Type of Walk: A demanding walk across peat moors; not suitable for days of poor visibility.

Map: OS Outdoor Leisure Map 21: South Pennines

Public transport: *Bus:* Service operated to Worsthorne by LAK.

Along the Borderline

The moors that lie to the east of Black Hameldon are traversed by the Pennine Way in one of its tougher stages, and anyone undertaking the Way will hereabouts get a good indication of what to expect of this walk. On a bright summer's day the circuit is a delight, but let the clouds gather and the skies darken, and moods will plummet along with hopes of ever reaching safety. Save this walk for a good day when the forecast is for sunshine throughout; it is for stout minds as well as legs.

The name Black Hameldon means *black-scarred hill*, and so it is. This ascent begins from the attractive village of Worsthorne, not far from Burnley, from where a splendid track, Gorple Road, an old packhorse route, races out of the village, bound for the moors. It begins beside the church of St John the Evangelist, and runs arrow-straight eastwards. Surfaced at first, the track soon degenerates into a rough surface, rising all the time to a level stretch beyond which it can be seen continuing ahead beside Smallshaw Clough.

Simply keep following this track as it presses on to reach the Gorple Stones, a large collection of gritstone boulders to the left of the track. As you approach the stones, leave the track at a collapsed

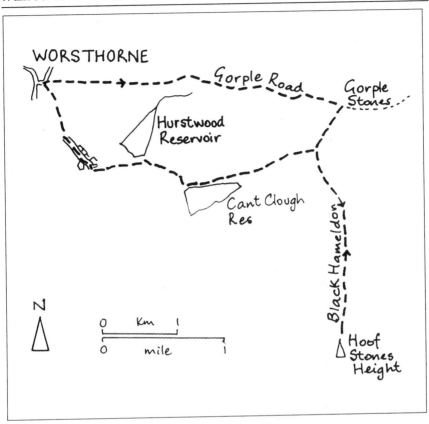

waymark, heading south-west across marshy ground to another prominent group of boulders, the Hare Stones. Just after Hare Stones note a small pile of stones beside the track: these mark the start of a path branching right into Rams Clough, the way you will return. From the stones a clear path heads roughly south to pull on to Black Hameldon's peaty slopes, continuing in often miry conditions to the more southerly summit of Hoof Stones Height, the highest point of Black Hameldon.

Retreat from Hoof Stones Height to the pile of stones and there turn left, descending through tussock grass to cross a stream, and rising beyond to meet a more pronounced path marked by poles. If you follow these they will lead you through an undulating, rolling moorland landscape of considerable beauty to reach Cant Clough

Reservoir, close by which a bench makes a convenient place for a breather.

Press on beside the reservoir in-flow, and go left on a broad track, through a wall, to keep on between a wall and the water's edge. Further on the track goes back through the wall, at a gate, and continues to the dam. On reaching the dam, turn right up a concrete track, and follow this to reach Hurstwood Reservoir.

As you approach Hurstwood Reservoir, the track forks. The main track keeps right, but you should branch left, near an electricity pylon, to go for a gate (yellow-topped waymark nearby). Through the gate you enter a small plantation, and follow a path ahead to reach the reservoir access road. Turn left, and follow the road out to reach the village of Hurstwood, which has an attractive hall. At a T-junction, near a telephone box, go left and follow the road out of the village.

About 100m/yds after the last house on the right, turn right at a gap stile (signposted to Worsthorne). Keep forward beside a wall to enter a short walled section before crossing into open pasture with the tower of Worsthorne church directly ahead. Aim for this, and at a kissing gate you are led on to a paved pathway that takes you back into the village.

Walk 40: Thieveley Pike and Black Scout

Start/Finish: Holme Chapel. Limited parking, use a roadside lay-by 200m/yds south-east along the A646

Distance: 7 miles (11km)

Height gain: 1395ft (425m)

Walking time: 4-5 hours

Type of Walk: Fairly energetic with two rough climbs over peaty moorland.

Map: OS Outdoor Leisure Map 21: South Pennines

Public transport: *Bus:* YOR and ELM run services to Holme Chapel.

Cliviger Circle

En route between Todmorden and Burnley, the hills of East Lancashire constrict to fashion the Cliviger Gorge, which is overlooked by the craggy fringe of Thieveley Scout and above which the moors rise to the summit of Thieveley Pike. The views are unrivalled in this part of the county and combine both urban and rural settings. Across the valley the long ridge of Black Scout is another tempting walking area, combined here with the ascent of Thieveley Pike to give a fine circular tour based on the village of Holme Chapel.

From the lay-by walk back towards Holme Chapel, go past the Ram Inn, and as far as a telephone box near which you turn left on to a signposted track. Go down this and shortly pass beneath a railway bridge. Go forward to a waymarked post, turn right and keep on for a few strides to a gate at the junction of two collapsing walls. Beyond start ascending in a westerly direction, climbing steeply, curving leftwards to a set of stone steps at the end of a wall on Stone House Edge. Go through a gap in the wall.

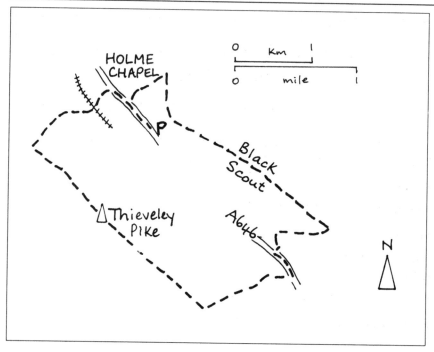

Press on in the same direction to reach the buildings at Cow Side.
Turn left and go along beside a wall, and through a gate. Keep
forward to and beyond another gate before crossing Black Clough,
then rising obliquely right on a track through tussock grass and
passing above an area of opencast coal mining to reach the trig on
the summit. You will need to abandon the track in order to reach
the summit. The view, almost an entire unobstructed 360 panorama
of East Lancashire, is magnificent and embraces all the surrounding
towns and villages and distant Pendle Hill, as well as Ingleborough
and Pen y Ghent in the Yorkshire Dales.

Thieveley Pike was one of a chain of beacon hills that linked
Pendle Hill and Blackstone Edge, along with many more similar
heights throughout the length and breadth of northern England.

Cross the stile over the summit ridge fence and take to a track that
heads south-east towards the expanse of Heald Moor. At the top of
Heald Moor, follow a Burnley Way signpost that sends you off in a
north-easterly direction descending steeply above Green's Clough.

Down below aim for a stile in a wall, beyond which the on-going path meets a stony track. Turn left, going downhill with it to a gate near a ruined building. Pass through the gate and on to another track descending through bracken, before heading right to reach a bull-dozed road heading down into Chatham Hill Plantation. Follow this to meet the A646 Burnley road.

Turn left along the road for about 300m/yds, and there leave it for a farm road that goes round a small lake to reach Dean Farm. At the farm, cross a stile and pursue a green road up the hillside beyond, ultimately to reach the ridge of Black Scout. Keep a wall to your left and turn left along the ridge, with the unsightly vision of the wind turbines on Warcock Hill, only previously seen at a distance, now much closer.

After a little over a mile (2km) use a stile to cross to the other side of the wall and stay with the wall as it passes beneath electricity pylons. Then turn half left, going down a reed-lined sunken way to another stile. From it head north-west to join a green road that later becomes a stony farm track. Turn right along the track and go in front of a farmhouse. At the end of the track, beyond a stile, a path leads you on to reach the eastern edge of Green Clough Wood before descending once more to cross the clough itself on a footbridge.

Across the clough, rise through bracken, returning to the boundary of the woodland and crossing two fields to reach a walled track that sends you descending hastily back to Holme Chapel. Turn left along the road to return to your starting point.

Walk 41: Blackstone Edge

Start/Finish: Ealees Car Park, Hollingworth Lake. GR.939153

Distance: 6¼ miles (10km)

Height gain: 1080ft (330m)

Walking time: 4-4½ hours

Type of Walk: A fine moorland walk that has been a firm favourite since Victorian times.

Map: OS Outdoor Leisure Map 21: South Pennines

Public transport: *Bus:* Numerous bus services operate through nearby Littleborough.

Down there is Yorkshire. Down there is Lancashire

In the good old days the ridge of Blackstone Edge formed the boundary between Yorkshire and Lancashire, which is all the justification I need for including this splendid walk in this book. What was Yorkshire, however, became first West Yorkshire and then Calderdale; and what was Lancashire became Greater Manchester, and even that has now ceased to exist as a metropolitan county. But for me, and many others, this will always be Lancashire.

The ascent of Blackstone Edge has been popular since Victorian times, and in spring or summer, when the ridge is aired by gentle breezes, you can enjoy long, leg-swinging days tramping the moors, seeking out peaceful, sheltered corners, listening to the song of the skylark and the call of buzzard and curlew overhead, much as the Victorians would have done.

The walk begins at Hollingworth Lake, a compensation reservoir, but better known among Victorians as a source of pleasure and entertainment. Not a lot has changed, and most weekends will find the lake and its environs crowded with visitors.

From the car park take a broad track heading north-east. When

Hollingworth Lake, Greater Manchester (Julie Meech)

this veers right, leave it for a paved way across a field. Cross a narrow footbridge and keep on, passing through gates, until a minor road is reached near Lane Foot Farm. A neat, wooded valley runs left here to Ealees, and another, less immediately obvious, to the right of the great prow of hill directly ahead of us. To reach it, go left, beside a stream, for a short distance to a yellow waymark that directs you up a flight of steps towards the farm, before the path veers across the spine of the ridge into the next valley. Another wooden bridge takes you across a stream.

Soon you reach a golf course, with the main track going left around it. But here you pass through a gate to follow a path across the course, soon becoming a broad track along the edge of one of the fairways. Visible throughout virtually the whole of the walk, the objective, Blackstone Edge, is an impressive, craggy frieze along the skyline. Once beyond the golf course, go left on a metalled roadway to the tiny settlement of Lydgate on Blackstone Edge Old Road.

At Lydgate turn right, passing by the houses, to follow an undu-

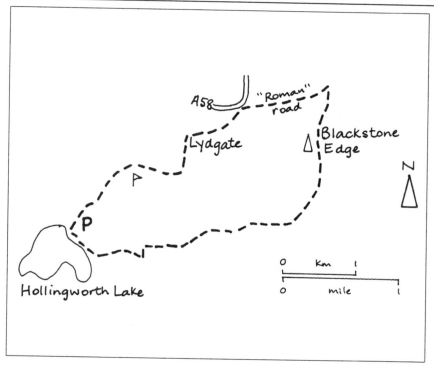

lating path beside a wall, and almost touching the nearby A58. Here you begin the steepest part of the walk, pursuing the famous 'Roman road' of Blackstone Edge. The earliest suggestion that this route might be of Roman origin was made by William Stukely in 1725, with many subsequent opinions supporting or rejecting this claim. Whether it is, is unlikely ever to be satisfactorily resolved.

Part way up the Roman road you encounter the Pennine Way, that symbol of man's freedom to roam, coming down as it crosses Blackstone Edge on its way north to the Halifax road. At this highest point of the road stands a prominent stone, the Aiggin Stone (pronounced "Aijin"), inscribed with a Latin cross and the initials "IT". Again the suggestion is that the stone is of Roman origin.

Between the Aiggin Stone and Blackstone Edge, the Pennine Way (southbound) guides you across an area of peat and gritstone. The summit trig, awkward to attain, is perched on one of many outcropping gritstone boulders. The largest outcrop has attracted the name

"Robin Hood's Bed". The name of Robin Hood is not confined to the area around Nottingham, but occurs quite frequently throughout the southern Pennines and the Peak, which was formerly part of the huge medieval hunting forest of Sherwood.

From the summit of Blackstone Edge the Pennine Way heads for the trans-Pennine motorway (M62). But you ignore this and remain instead with the rocky escarpment of the Edge until the opportunity presents itself to descend across untracked ground towards the mound of Clegg Moor. To be sure of finding the right line, you can take a more or less westerly direction, and will then in due course encounter the man-made leat, Broad Head Drain, which you can follow until it loses itself on a shallow marshy col. At this point an initially indistinct path traces a line across the edge of Clegg Moor. A short-lived line of cairns points you in the right direction. A small pool, Dry Mere, hides in a grassy basin, and the nearby heathery slopes are an ideal spot to relax and while away some time before committing yourself to the final stage of the walk, which will take you back to the company of the day-trippers sauntering along the lakeside promenade.

Continue, then, down the rough track passing Dry Mere to reach a broad, graded track extending, right, back to Lydgate. Cross this, and bear left on a grassy trod until it descends in a broad sweep to a stony track leading us to the cottages at Syke. It is but a short stroll along a pleasant country lane to regain the lakeshore a short distance south of the Ealees Car Park.

Walk 42: Saddleworth Edges

Start/Finish: Binn Green car park. GR.018044

Distance: 8 miles (13km)

Height gain: 835ft (255m)

Walking time: 3½-4 hours

Type of Walk: Easy approach alongside the reservoir, leading to a rocky clough and a short, grassy pull to the edge walk proper. A good path leads round the rim of the plateaux, with splendid airy views.

Map: OS Landranger 1:50 000 series Sheet 110: Sheffield and Huddersfield

Public transport: *Bus:* YOR operate services that pass the Binn Green car park.

On the Edge

At the northern limits of the Peak National Park, the Pennine Way crosses the Wessenden and Saddleworth Moors, before heading on towards Blackstone Edge and Stoodley Pike, the moors that will forever be associated with the Brontë sisters. Although the peat bogs of the moors have now largely been tamed, so far as Pennine Wayfarers are concerned, they used to enjoy an unenviable reputation for difficult and messy walking.

Yet only a short distance west, where the plateau drops to the densely-populated valleys, is to be found one of the most endearing walks in the whole of the Peak, known locally as the Saddleworth Edges. It is a place of great beauty in a rough-hewn way, focused on a string of reservoirs, and represents for the people of eastern Lancashire an entire Lake District on their own doorsteps.

The reservoirs Greenfield, Yeoman Hey and Dove Stone are very popular at weekends throughout the year, though few visitors un-

The Trinnacle (Saddleworth Edges)

dertake more than a stroll beside them, leaving the grand balcony of the Saddleworth Edges free for more energetic souls.

The walk begins at the Binn Green car park on the A635, just out of Greenfield. A flight of steps leads down into a small copse of conifers, and to a squeeze stile giving access to the reservoir road. The route turns left here and descends to Yeoman Hey Reservoir, constructed in 1880, and visited 101 years later by the King of Tonga, Taufa'ahau Tupou IV.

Follow the service track around the left (western) side of the reservoir. Above rises a conifer plantation, known as Bill o'Jack's, after the former innkeeper, William Bradbury, of the Moor Cock Inn, until 1935 to be found along the Holmfirth road. He and his father Jack met an untimely death in 1832 at the hands of unknown assailants, and were buried at Saddleworth church.

Continue, in company with a relief channel, until you reach Greenfield Reservoir (1903). As you leave the reservoir behind you enter Greenfield Brook, a place of delightful cascades frowned down upon by the dark cliffs of Ravenstones, prominent among which is the curious tower of The Trinnacle, perhaps the most impressive feature along the Edges.

A short distance further on Greenfield Brook divides into Holme Clough (left) and Birchin Clough (right). Close by, a dark tunnel captures the waters of Birchin Clough and sends them tumbling underground to the Dove Stone Reservoir. Do not explore!

Cross the top of the tunnel to follow the course of Birchin Clough, a short, scrambly route, crossing and recrossing the stream with varying degrees of difficulty according to the levels of rainfall, but eventually entering a narrow section above a small cascade. The path, much less obvious now, presses on along the line of the brook, but it can be abandoned almost anywhere to strike up the hillside on the right to a conspicuous path doubling back along the line of Birchin Clough. From this elevated vantage point a spectacularly expansive panorama unfolds across the bleak and barren tops of the Saddleworth Moors. It is quite unsuspected from below, with wild and rocky valleys reminiscent of remote Scottish glens.

As you follow the edge path so the rock architecture improves

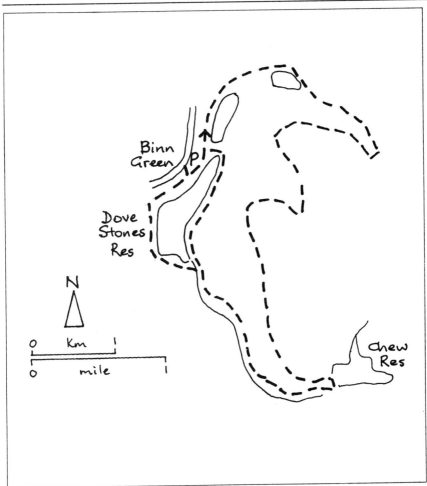

until quite soon you reach The Trinnacle, a fine free-standing pillar of rock, split, as its name suggests into three. Walkers with a good head for heights will have no difficulty reaching its highest point, but getting down is for some more awkward than going up.

The Trinnacle marks the true start of the edge walk, and from here a good path wanders onwards in splendid airy fashion to the next objective, Ashway Cross, a memorial to a Member of Parliament killed in a shooting accident.

From Ashway Cross the path bends to cross Dovestone Clough before resuming its progress along the edge above another fine escarpment of gritstone faces. Further on yet another memorial is encountered, this time to two climbers killed in 1972 in the Dolomites, and beyond that is to be found a unique dwelling, Bramley's Cot, constructed against a face of rock in an ingenious way. There was a time when it was sufficiently complete to see service as a shooting lodge.

Continue along the marginal path with a few unavoidable patches of peat to contend with, noting the obvious gully across the valley, Wilderness Gully, scene in 1963 of one of England's largest avalanches, in which two climbers were killed. The path continues along the edge until finally you reach Chew Reservoir, constructed in 1912, the highest reservoir in England, though Cow Green Reservoir in Teesdale contests the claim.

By following the reservoir service road a speedy descent to the valley bottom may be made, to be greeted in summer by shoals of would-be adventurers gathered around the dam of Dove Stone Reservoir and along its shores. From the dam it is only a short walk back to the Binn Green picnic area using either the broad path beside the reservoir, or ascending to a stile above the unusual circular overflow to gain a path back to the start.

Walk 43: Around Pleasington

Start/Finish: Witton Park car park. GR.663271

Distance: 6 miles (10km)

Height gain: 410ft (125m)

Walking time: 3 hours

Type of Walk: Easy walking through woodland and a mainly rural landscape.

Map: OS Explorer 19: West Pennine Moors

Public transport: *Bus:* RIB and BOR run numerous services along the A674, stopping near Witton Park. *Rail:* Pleasington, enabling the walk to start from there.

Pleasant in the Extreme

Lying a couple of miles to the west of Blackburn, the parish of Pleasington is an ancient one, with records taking it back into the thirteenth century, and probably much earlier. There is a suggestion in its name, that the scholarly debate at levels far higher than my comprehension, that it is of Anglo-Saxon origin. Arthur Mee, writing about Lancashire, said of Pleasington that it stood, "On a green hill a mile or two from smoky Blackburn [with] an old hall, now a farmhouse, with grey walls and gables seen against a background of trees."

The area visited by this walk is one that speaks much about the old families of Lancashire: the Butlers, who held Pleasington Hall; the Feildens, who in 1800 created what is now Witton Country Park; and the Hoghton family of Hoghton Tower, who were sufficiently elevated in the nobility to entertain royalty. The landscape crossed by the walk is varied, and combines attractive woodlands rich in birdlife with more pastoral settings that, on the edge of a large city like Blackburn, many will find surprising.

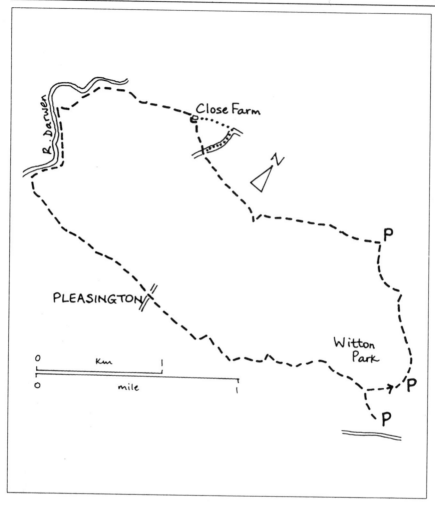

From the car park go clockwise round the athletics track (scene
of numerous humiliations during my athletics years) and pass to the
right of the sports pavilion, which sells refreshments for those who
might want them on their return. At the rear of the pavilion turn
right on to a surfaced track flanked by rhododendron bushes. This
soon reaches a metal gate near a small car park. Immediately after
the gate turn left beside a fence to follow a path through trees and
with a fence on the left, leading a short way on into oak, birch and

beech woodland on a surfaced pathway. Just after a sign for a path to Billinge Wood, go left across a footbridge spanning a small stream, then continuing higher into the woodland, rising gradually on a path that is stepped, rather hugely in places. Keep on until you meet open pasture at a gate. Cross two fields (waymarked) to reach Under Billinge Lane, which as its name suggests lies at the foot of Billinge Hill, a locally popular woodland viewpoint. Access to the lane is by a stone stile.

Turn left along the lane, then right in about twenty paces through an open gate into the woodland. As you pass through the gate go left on an undulating path. When the path forks, branch right (in effect ahead) and continue climbing. When you pass a white post with the figure 7 on it, keep left, soon to leave the woodland at the corner of another car park. Go immediately left on reaching the car park, over a low stile at the end of a wall.

Continue ahead on a broad grassy track, with the Darwen Moors rising in the distance to the left, adjoined by Winter Hill and the Anglezarke Moors, while far away, half right, you can pick out Blackpool Tower on the horizon. Cross the remains of a grassed-over wall and keep on heading for a small hillock ahead. Cross a wooden step stile just before the hillock and then continue over the hump and down the other side. Pass through the remains of another wall to reach a fence (gate/stile). Just to the left at this point is Butler's Delph Quarry, named after the family that used to live at Pleasington Hall. Stay close to the quarry fence, and this will guide you down to two more step stiles, beyond the second of which you descend through heather, bracken and birch to a lane.

Go left, and then immediately right on a signposted footpath, but after about 50m/yds leave the path for a less distinct one curving right through scrub to a low stile at the edge of open pasture. Keep ahead across the field, beside trees that are all that remain of an old hedgerow, to reach a gateway. Ignore the path branching left, and keep ahead following the line of trees, mainly holly and hawthorn, on your right, to reach another gate, just before which you meet a broad access track. Go ahead on the track to reach the lane linking Pleasington and Billinge End.

On reaching the lane, cross it, and go forward along a field edge towards Close Farm. As you approach Close Farm (Beware dogs!) the public footpath appears to have been lost in a garden. The continuation then involves going to the left of the buildings to reach a hedgerow going left. If you are not happy with this uncertainty you can, on reaching the Pleasington lane, go right to a junction and then follow the access track, left, to Close Farm.

Follow the hedgerow down the field. When the hedgerow ends, a grassy track continues ahead across a shallow depression before curving left slightly to reach the top edge of a wooded dean. Cross a stile and keep ahead on a green path to go down into the dean, climbing on the other side along a shelf between woodland on your right and a low bank above you on your left. Now follow the top edge of the woodland, ignoring the tempting remains of a bridge and a conduit away to the left, and soon you descend to meet the River Darwen. As you reach the river go left past a wooden scout hut, and ahead along a muddy track to reach Lower Park Farm. Beside the farm buildings cross a stile that leads in a few strides through a wall gap to the front of the farmhouse. Go in front of it and walk ahead to rejoin the river. Here do not cross the river but turn left along a track, with the river on your right. Hoghton Tower now looms above you in its wooded shelter, high on the right.

Present day Hoghton Tower was built during the time of Elizabeth I on the site of the ancestral home of the de Hoghton family since the early fourteenth century, and it has endured "a history of pageantry and romance, fighting and failure, richness and squalor, revival and decay". (Mee) It was erected by Thomas Hoghton in 1565, but it was his successor, Sir Richard, who, in 1617, entertained King James I to three days of feasting during which, in a moment of merriment, the king is said to have knighted a particular splendid loin of beef, making it sirloin for all perpetuity. The hall is still in the de Hoghton family, and occasionally open to the public.

When the track forks, branch right to stay with the river to a single-arched bridge. Here cross a stile and turn left along a track, soon bending left as it meets a wall. After 70m/yds cross a stile giving on to Pleasington golf course. Keep ahead beside the wall (left) to a stile beyond which the wall is replaced with a fence (right). This guides you on over a small hillock then to go forward in the same direction to reach the village of Pleasington, which you can locate ahead by the twin pinnacles of its Roman Catholic church. The walk enters the village along a broad track leading into a modern housing estate, before debouching on Victoria Road next to the Butler's Arms and the church. Walkers arriving by train to Pleasington will begin and end the walk at this point.

The Roman Catholic church (St Mary and St John the Baptist) was built in 1816-19 for John Frances Butler of Pleasington Hall by John Palmer of Manchester. It is known as Pleasington Priory, and has many features that copy the style of the thirteenth century, particularly the lofty arcades and arches. The building has a great many buttresses and battlements, an attractive clerestory with many windows below a massive balustrade, and numerous figures, faces and statues.

Cross the road and go onward along a track that runs on to meet a narrower path, fenced on both sides, that guides you onwards, eventually down a sandy ravine, to reach the edge of playing fields. Go left and right, around the first football pitch to rejoin the River Darwen at a couple of bridges, one modern, the other Butler's Bridge, and rather more ancient.

Turn left on reaching the river, keeping it on your right and passing more football pitches. Ignore a tempting footbridge, and follow the field edge until you can go right, down steps to a stile giving on to the edge of Witton Park. Follow an obvious path across the next field to a stile at the edge of woodland. Cross this and turn immediately right over a small footbridge, and then left. Now in the distance you can see the sports pavilion and athletics track. Head for this, and the car park beyond.

Walk 44: Darwen Moor West

Start/Finish: Crookfield Road car park. GR.665191

Distance: 8 miles (12.5km)

Height gain: Very little

Walking time: 3 hours

Type of Walk: Mostly on good paths, with wide moorland views.

Map: OS Explorer 19: West Pennine Moors

Public transport: *Bus:* DCS, HOR and GMB operate services that pass the turning to the Crookfield car park. Some run only from Bolton to Belmont, so start the walk at Belmont.

The Belmont Road

In the days when Liverpool Waterworks Department's policies meant that access to the West Pennine Moors was something you wished for, but could do little about, much of the land that now enjoys a freedom to roam access was strictly a 'no-go' area. There are still many places where keeping to the right of way, which many walkers and writers see as a restriction of freedom rather than an expansion, is still necessary. This walk, however, manages to spend a good deal of its time on Access Land, where there is a true freedom to roam, and begins at the southern edge of Tockholes, and treks south to Belmont before returning along the wide moors of Spitlers Edge and Redmonds Edge.

Start at the Crookfield Road Car Park on the back road that runs from the A675 to Tockholes village, and go left along a path beside the road to a left bend. Leave the road here, over a stile on the right beside a gate, to set off along a broad track racing south across the western edge of Darwen Moor. Before long the track passes the ruins of Lower Pasture Barn Farm, and keeps on along a section known as Catherine Edge.

Belmont Church and the "Blue Lagoon"

The route presses on easily, with the untidy clutter of Winter Hill looming massively ahead. Belmont Reservoir, with its island, endeavours valiantly to draw the eye, and is a favoured haunt of a wide range of birdlife, though summer months will see it dotted with the colourful sails of boats.

Keep going, striding purposefully along part of a fine route known as the Witton Weavers' Way, until you reach a track on the right leading down to Higher Pasture House Farm, and turn down it (over a stile), soon to pass beside farm buildings. As you do, at a gate, turn left in front of the farmhouse, then follow the descending farm access to meet a minor lane near the dam of Belmont Reservoir. Turn right and cross the dam, rising to the right at the far end to meet the A675.

Head right along the A675 for about 100m/yds, then turn left over a stile and along the access to Ward's Cote Farm. Pass the farm buildings and go left for a short distance to a low stile over a fence on the right. The next section is often unclear on the ground and

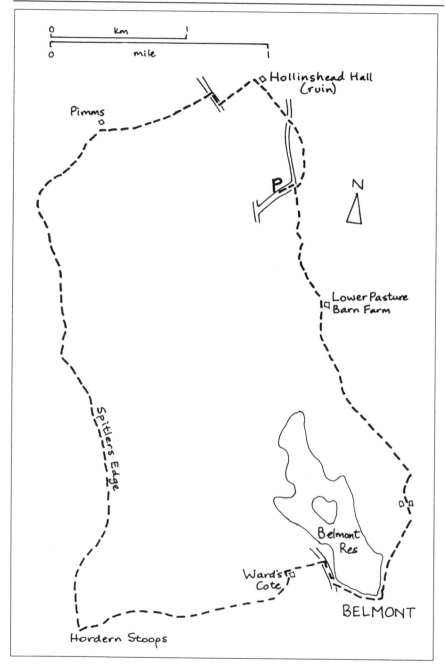

boggy, with only sheep tracks to aid progress, but generally head slightly left towards a wall, keeping parallel with it until you intersect a path ascending from Belmont.

Now you can follow this clear and wide path roughly westwards across Sharples Higher End, high above Rivington Road, until eventually it feeds out to the road. Keep along the road for about 150m/yds then leave it, heading right, parallel with a fence, to a stile that gives on to the only steepness of the day, a brief pull on to the southern end of Spitlers Edge. Once this little nonsense is over, you can march across the moors on a path close by a wall, and only moving away from it as the paved section of this route is reached beyond the high point of Spitlers Edge. Follow the paved slabs across once-notorious, now tamed, peat groughs to reach a fence near the base of Great Hill.

The path from the fence bears right (not up on to Great Hill) into tussock grass, amid which it soon loses its way, leaving you to battle on in the general direction of derelict Pimms Farm for the short distance until you meet the broad track descending from Great Hill. This steers you right to cross a stream, beyond which you climb to a fence, and a path leading out to the A675 near Piccadilly Farm.

Turn right on reaching the road and walk up to a path (signposted Hollinshead Hall) on the left. Take this, and at a path junction bear right to visit the ruins of Hollinshead Hall, the former manor house of the township of Tockholes.

The ruins of Hollinshead Hall that remain today are of eighteenth and nineteenth-century origin, though there is evidence that the Hollinshead family owned a manor house, perhaps on this site, as long ago as the fourteenth century. The hall was once very extensive, but a large part of it was demolished by the owner, John Hollinshead, in 1776, following which he re-built the hall on a less imposing scale. During the early years of the nineteenth century the hall was often the focus of many social occasions hosted by the Brock-Hollinsheads, a long-established Lancashire family. In 1845 the hall was sold to a Darwen mill owner, Eccles Sharrock, who seems to have largely neglected the condition of the property because by the end of the century it was in disrepair. The hall was eventually demolished when Liverpool Corporation acquired the land for water catchment; much of the stonework went into the construction of walls in the area and a few cottages in Belmont village.

The scale of the latter-day hall is evident from the remains, though the feature that arouses most interest is the well house, which is still largely intact and has been restored in recent times. Such well houses were used for a number of purposes, usually the storage of dairy produce or a garden summer house. This one is said to be haunted in spite of claims that its true purpose was to house a 'holy' spring or wishing well, which are traditionally venerated in many parts of the country. This was a pagan tradition that was often later christianised, giving rise to an era of pilgrimage, when people would make journeys to visit these wells in search of relief for a miscellany of complaints. There are certainly records that this was the case at Hollinshead.

Resuming the walk, keep on up the track past Hollinshead Hall to meet the Tockholes road, cross it, and take to a concessionary bridleway that loops southwards and saves you having to dice with speeding traffic on the road. The path gradually turns round to descend to gates, to rejoin the road at the bend where you first left it at the start of the walk. Now just retrace your steps to the car park.

Walk 45: Jumbles and Wayoh Reservoirs

Start/Finish: Waterfold Car Park, off Bradshaws Road (A676). GR.736140

Distance: 6 miles (10km)

Height gain: 625ft (190m)

Walking time: 3-4 hours

Type of Walk: Easy walking on good paths.

Map: OS Explorer 19: West Pennine Moors

Public transport: *Bus:* RIB, ROS and BPT operate along Bradshaw Road, from which it is a walk of about 400m/yds to the Waterfold car park.

Turton Trails

This pleasant circular walk around the Jumbles and Wayoh Reservoirs also facilitates a visit to Turton Tower, an attractive old manor house, set amid beautiful grounds, and in part dating from the fifteenth century. There is much to see along this walk, and both the Information Centre and Turton Tower staff will provide you with information before you set off especially of the opening times of the Tower.

Begin from the Waterfold Car Park Information Centre, reached from the A676 – Bradshaws Road. Turn left and walk through the main car park, following the footpath down the side of the embankment at the southern end of the reservoir, and descend steps to a stile at the end of a bridge. Take the path to the left, towards Ousel Nest Field Cottage, and follow the curve of the hedgerow to the right until the path meets Grange Road at another stile. Turn right.

A short way along Grange Road a signpost points up to the Ousel Nest Car Park, but ignore this and continue along Grange Road to

Turton Tower

pass through the gates of Grange Farm, walking on along an avenue of trees, alternating lime and horse chestnut. At the farm go through the stables and out on to the reservoir path, and continue past the Civil Service Sailing Club buildings, and up Horrobin Lane.

At the top of Horrobin Lane turn right and cross Chapeltown Road (B6391), which can be quite busy. Follow the road, uphill, to the turning to Turton Tower, on the left.

Turton Tower was originally a pele tower, probably dating from the fifteenth century. Towards the end of the sixteenth century, William Orrell refashioned and extended the living quarters, though much of the ornate timbering is the work of Joseph (James?) Kay, a cotton spinner from Preston, who acquired the estate in 1835. During the Civil War (1642-49) the estate was owned by the High Sheriff of Lancashire, Humphrey Chetham of Manchester.

Go past the tower and soon you will cross over the Blackburn to Bolton railway line, then bearing right beside a stream as the route sweeps out on to moorland pastures. Now follow a clearly defined

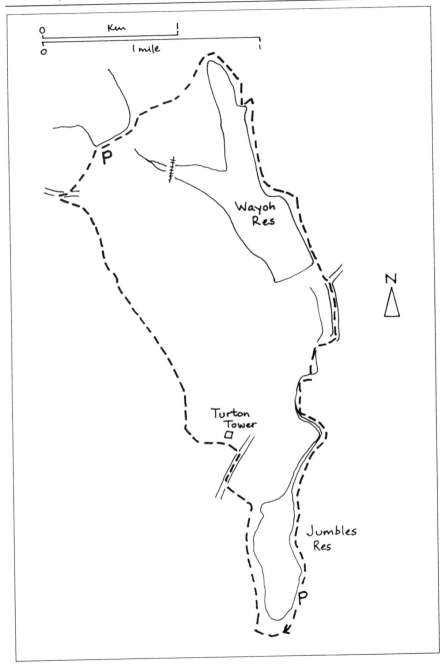

way past Clough House Farm, continuing until you meet Greens Arms Road (B6391). At the road turn right for about 80m/yds, and then branch left, following a path down to the Batridge car park near the dam of the Turton and Entwistle Reservoir. Off to your right you can see Wayoh Reservoir, around which the walk now circles. The Wayoh Reservoir became functional in 1876 as a compensation reservoir, supplying water for the industrial concerns in the Bradshaw valley.

From the car park walk to the far side of Turton and Entwistle embankment, continuing ahead along Overshores Road to reach the Strawberry Duck, and then cross the railway line. At a small stile on the left a short way on, cross into a field and follow a path through mixed woodland to reach two wooden bridges at the northernmost end of Wayoh Reservoir. Now the path continues through woodland down the eastern side of the reservoir.

This is a particularly important area for bird watching, and almost 150 species have been recorded here at all times of the year. The water area in particular gives some fine sightings, such as whooper swans, tufted duck, pochard and grebes, while the water margins host some interesting species of plant, many of them rare, so do not pick them – in any case, it is unlawful to uproot wild flowers.

When you reach Hob Lane, cross it and follow a path around the edge of the main reservoir. The path continues pleasantly, and climbs to a fine vantage point near the south-eastern corner of the reservoir. Beyond the farmland on your left the row of houses you see stand along the Roman road known as Watling Street, which linked forts at Manchester and Ribchester.

The path then descends to the reservoir at the corner of the Wayoh embankment, and from there you leave the reservoir and press on in the same direction to reach the road at the southern end of Edgworth. Walk down the road to Turton Bottoms. Cross Bradshaw Brook on the road bridge, and about 100m/yds further on go left on a path that takes you back down to recross the brook. Now all that remains is for you to follow Bradshaw Brook southwards. The valley gradually opens out as you approach Jumbles Reservoir before continuing down the eastern side to return to your starting point.

Walk 46: Rivington to White Coppice via the Woodland Trail

Start/Finish: Rivington village. GR.626145

Distance: 8 miles (13km)

Height gain: Negligible

Walking time: Allow 4 hours

Type of Walk: Generally easy on good paths/trails, but occasionally muddy.

Map: OS Explorer 19: West Pennine Moors

Public transport: *Bus:* RIB run services to Horwich, some 2 miles (3km) distant.

By Zarke and Woodland Ways

With ample parking in the many side lanes that branch from the main road through Rivington, there is no excuse for obstructing the main, and often very busy, carriageway.

Begin from the small village green at Rivington, taking a moment first to inspect the stocks that held the miscreants of yesteryear. Keep the stocks on your left, descend a brief flight of steps in a retaining wall and cross the road to a kissing gate. Beyond the gate lies a wide, sloping meadow, with a grassy path keeping close by the right-hand fenceline to reach a longer set of steps leading down across a stream to a path going right between fences and along the line of Dean Brook. Stay with this path to its end at a stile, at a junction with a broader trail.

Go sharp left here, crossing Dean Brook, and ascending gently for a short distance to reach another broad track, on the right, running arrow-straight to the embankment of Yarrow Reservoir, constructed in 1875. Follow this track, strolling pleasantly along a walled lane with good views to the left and right. Ignore a branching track

White Coppice

descending left (you will return this way), but keep on to cross an overflow linking Yarrow with Anglezarke Reservoir below. Just before the overflow bridge, one of the capping stones in the wall on the right has been carved, by a reservoir construction worker, into the likeness of a face, allegedly the works foreman. It is not easy to find because over the years it has been rather defaced.

Beyond the bridge, the track continues through gorse-bearing embankments to give a fine view, right, over Yarrow Reservoir to the distant pincushion of Winter Hill and its clutter of masts. Eventually, the track runs out to a road, and here you turn left, descending the road with care to a junction. Turn right, still following a road, until, at the first opportunity, you can leave it, left, to pursue the Anglezarke Woodland Trail.

There are a number of possibilities to effect circular tours along the trail, but for our purposes begin by keeping left, through a gate near the entrance to the car park. This takes you down a surfaced track above Anglezarke Reservoir and past side paths that lead, for the curious, into Leicester Mill Quarry. This is one of the quarries that provided stone for building and road construction throughout the north west, indeed, many of the streets of Manchester are paved with stone from the Anglezarke quarries.

Further on, the track swings round to move round a small inlet below High Bullough Reservoir, constructed in 1850 to supply water

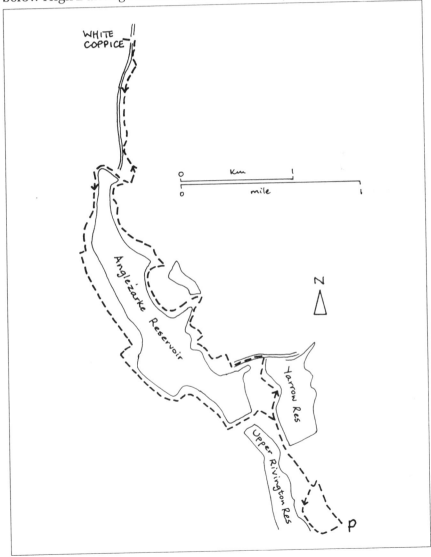

to Chorley. As the road climbs on the other side, leave it, left by a signboard, to follow a delightful woodland path around the edges of Brook House Plantation. The on-going route is never in doubt, and finally descends to a junction of pathways, where the Woodland Trail turns right to return to the car park. Here, leave the Trail, and go left on a path that heads across meadows at the northern end of Anglezarke Reservoir, at one point climbing along a narrow path above steep embankments before finally running out to meet a road at a gate/stile.

Go left down the road, and immediately leave it at a gate, on the right. The broad path beyond curves across rough pasture on the western fringe of Anglezarke Moor, and, if followed faithfully, ignoring diversions, will lead you to the bridge over The Goyt that gives access to the charming village of White Coppice and its cricket field, beside which refreshments are often available.

To return, first retrace your steps to the road, and there turn right to cross around the northern end of Anglezarke Reservoir where a stile gives access to two footpaths, one of which, the one to follow, sets off down the western side of the reservoir, through pleasant woodland that is often alive with birdsong. The path is very muddy in places, but finally rises to a stile over a fence, beyond which the onward route is not immediately obvious. Go ahead, and slightly left, to reach a broad track, running left for about half a mile to the group of modernised houses at Kays Farm. When you meet their access road, turn right and walk out to a back lane.

Go left along the lane for about 400m/yds until you can leave it, left, to follow a path, initially wet, around a small headland – a splendid place for a rest, overlooking the reservoir and the quarries beyond. Continue on a good path to reach the road that crosses between Anglezarke and Upper Rivington reservoirs.

Cross between the reservoirs, and at the far end, as the road bends, leave through a gate on the right to follow a path that curves up beside the weirs of the Yarrow overflow, soon to reach the broad Yarrow track used on the outward walk. Follow this, right, to its end, and there go right, ultimately to swing round to meet the main Rivington road. Turn left, and walk up the road to the village green.

Walk 47: Great Hill and Spitler's Edge from White Coppice

Start/Finish: White Coppice. GR.618191

Distance: 7 miles (12km)

Height gain: 850ft (260m)

Walking time: 4-5 hours

Type of Walk: Refreshing, open moorland, but prone to bogginess. Comfortable wellies or stout walking boots advised.

Map: OS Explorer 19: West Pennine Moors

Public transport: There are no bus services to White Coppice, though RIB operate three services along the A674, from where White Coppice can be reached along country lanes.

Nightmare over

This grand tour of Anglezarke Moor used to be a nightmare if you attempted the north-south crossing of Redmonds and Spitler's Edge following prolonged rain. I well recall my fell-running days when the peaty clutches of Spitler's Edge in particular were a waist deep, training-day embrace from which I was relieved to extricate myself. Now all that is over. No, the peat hasn't gone, but the worst stretches have now been tamed by a yellow brick road that would please the Wizard of Oz, a long, serpentine trail of huge rock slabs that slides across the morass and consigns peat-laden memories to the file labelled 'Things I am happy to forget'.

White Coppice is a gradely place to begin, especially in spring, when the hedgerows and field margins are dotted with a bountiful selection of Lancashire's wild flowers. Its name is said to derive from the practice, still followed, of white-washing the cottages, many of which were weavers' dwellings. But do take care parking in and

On the Darwen Moors, with Great Hill in the background

around White Coppice, especially if there is a cricket match in progress, and try not to cause inconvenience to local residents.

Beyond the cricket field, commonly regarded as the most picturesque in Lancashire, if not quite of test standard, you cross the River Goyt and through a gate turn left on a stony track that soon starts ascending. Stay with this path as it bends and climbs towards an old quarry, skirting this on the left. The onward path is never in doubt as it lopes across the southern slopes of grassy Wheelton Moor, passing the remains of former farmsteads that once dotted these moors. Quite soon, the most prominent of these, Drinkwaters, comes into view, perched on a wide rock ledge and framed by a surrounding stand of trees against a backdrop of Great Hill itself.

A short way beyond Drinkwaters you cross a fence/stile and in so doing leave the open access area – a pioneering example for those who campaign for the freedom to roam everywhere on our British hills – for one in which it is important to keep to the paths. Alas, after rain, the top of Great Hill is a great mess, and rigid adherence

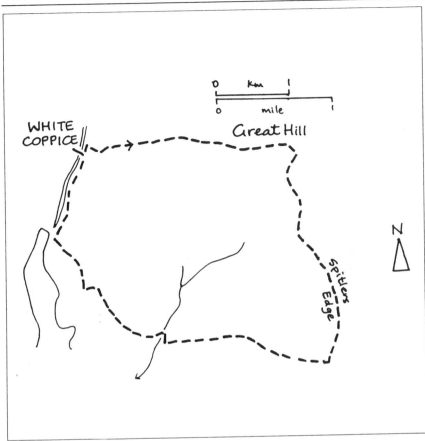

to this condition is certain to get your feet wet. But from the top of Great Hill, with the conspicuous Darwen Tower rising from blackened moors that were carelessly set alight during the tinder dry conditions of 1995, you can see, to the south-east, the long line of the new paved way.

If when you reach Great Hill you feel you have had enough, then I suggest you go back because at this point you are only about a quarter of the way into the walk, and though none of what follows is difficult, it does inject a certain weariness into your legs after a while.

Quite how to reach the paved trail from the top of Great Hill is not immediately obvious, but if you make a bee-line for it, you soon encounter a descending path that takes you down to another stile and the start of the paved section. Now the route description is easy, follow the paved way!

When the paved section ends, the going is not too bad. Another, short section of constructed path, this time using stones from the nearby collapsed wall, leads you on, until they too expire. Grassy slopes lead you down towards the Belmont road, but before reaching it, branch right on a narrow path that will take you first to the ruins of Higher Hempshaw's Farm and then Lower Hempshaw's. If you stick to what has become a farm access when you reach Lower Hempshaw's, this will loop you out across the moor to Simms Farm from where a broad track runs on, via stiles and gates, to reach Lead Mines Clough.

Lead Mines Clough is a fascinating place, first recorded as a lead mining area in 1692, following which the mines endured a chequered career until they finally closed in 1837. The shafts were filled in around 1930, as a way of finding employment for the people of Chorley. Some of the outstanding features of the area have been restored by the British Trust for Conservation Volunteers, and are worth taking time to explore. A leaflet is available from the Information Centre at Great House Barn in Rivington.

Descend into the clough, and cross the bridge that spans Limestone Brook, climbing the track beyond and following this over more stiles and/or through gates, finally to emerge at Jepson's Gate on to a back lane. Turn right, and follow the road down past Manor House and continuing to descend until near the northern tip of Anglezarke Reservoir you can go right, through a gate, to follow a broad track that will guide you back to the Goyt at White Coppice.

Walk 48: Darwen Moor

Start/Finish: Crookfield Road car park. GR.665191

Distance: 10 miles (16km)

Height gain: 820ft (250m)

Walking time: 4-5 hours

Type of Walk: Not suitable for poor visibility; good paths, but largely featureless moorland.

Map: OS Explorer 19: West Pennine Moors

Public transport: *Bus:* DCS operate between Blackburn and Belmont, enabling the start to be reached. Alternatively, the walk can be started in Darwen (see variant start at the end of the main route description).

Jubilee Tower Moors

The high moors above Darwen were once part of a large forest used for hunting, and later proved to hold hidden worth in the form of coal. Although the coal was not of high quality, it was mined from these moors for more than 300 years. Indeed, many of the tracks on the moors were formed by miners, who often worked in difficult conditions, hewing coal from narrow, one-man shafts only a few feet deep.

This circuit of the moors can begin just as easily in Darwen, but from the Crookfield Road car park on the Tockholes road, go left on a path beside the road, but only as far as the first bend, about 200m/yds away. Here leave the road by a stile/gate combination on the right, and follow a broad track beyond that sets off in the direction of Belmont and Winter Hill. A wall accompanies you for a while, but when this ends branch left, climbing easily, eventually to pass Higher Pasture Barn Farm. Beyond, as the track turns sharply left, keep ahead to the crest of the ascent. There cross a wall and keep on along the track, with a low wall on your right. Once across

Darwen Moors, with Darwen "Jubilee" Tower in the background

the highest ground of this stretch the track bends right and then left by two pillars, before running on down into the valley ahead to the ruins of Top o' th' Brow Farm.

Keep on past two stiles/gates, and just after the second such, turn left through a third gate into a field at the head of Cadshaw Valley. Though it seems hard to believe now, there was a time, during the nineteenth century, when more than 200 people lived and worked in this austere moorland valley.

Follow a wall up the field to a stile, and cross the next field heading half-left and then keep on, eventually to reach the top edge of a plantation. Follow a path beside a fence, and keep ahead over a number of stiles to reach the driveway of a white house, known locally as Lord's Hall. Turn right down the drive and near a cattle grid turn left beside a wall, continuing ahead to reach Darwen Tower and on the way branching first left then right at path junctions.

Darwen Tower, more correctly known as Jubilee Tower, was built by public subscription in 1897 to commemorate Queen Victoria's

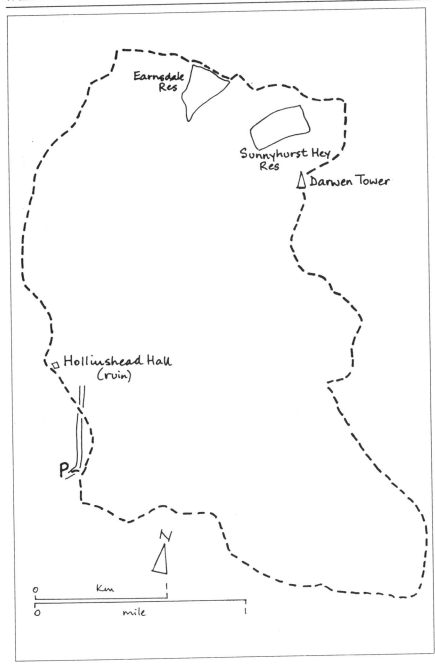

Earnsdale
Res

Sunnyhurst Hey
Res

Darwen Tower

Hollinshead Hall
(ruin)

P

N

0   Km   1

0   mile   1

Diamond Jubilee, and the opening of the Darwen Moors to the public after the mass trespasses of 1896, which pre-dated the much more vaunted trespass on Kinder Scout in Derbyshire by some 36 years.

From Darwen Tower head north-east and descend a wide track, branching left on the way on a track that passes north of Sunnyhurst Hey Reservoir to reach the lower Earnsdale Reservoir. Cross its dam, and keep on in the same direction to reach Tockholes Road. Turn left, cross the road, and in about 100m/yds take a path on the right into the Tockholes Plantation, and keep going, branching left to meet a more prominent track that comes in from the right. Turn right at a cross-path and go downhill to the reservoir, turning left there and continuing to cross the River Roddlesworth, better known locally as Rocky Brook.

Press on beside the river to reach and cross a stone bridge. Once over the bridge the track climbs steadily to reach a surfaced lane going left to the Tockholes road. Ignore this, and keep ahead, descending a little, soon to reach the ruins of Hollinshead Hall (see Walk 44 for more details about the hall). Keeping the ruins on your left, press on to meet the Tockholes road. Cross it to a gate, and follow the concessionary bridleway beyond as it loops right, above a plantation, before descending to reach the broad track used at the start of the walk. When you do, turn right to rejoin the road, and left to return to the car park.

Alternative start: This circuit may also be started from the Sunny-hurst Wood car park in Earnsdale Road, Darwen. Go down an alleyway, opposite the car park entrance, to Falcon Avenue. Turn left, and enter Sunnyhurst Wood. Pass a reservoir on the left, branch left over a stream, and then go right. Keep on along a wide path to reach a visitor centre. Go past a bandstand, then cross a bridge and stay with the stream until you leave the woodland park at a gate on to a track near the edge of Earnsdale Reservoir, where the above description continues.

Walk 49: Winter Hill and Lever Park

Start/Finish: Car park, Lever Park. GR.635129

Distance: 9 miles (14.5km)

Height gain: 1035ft (315m)

Walking time: 4-5 hours

Type of Walk: Generally easy, on good trails throughout.

Map: OS Explorer 19: West Pennine Moors

Public transport: *Bus:* RIB run services through nearby Horwich.

Folly, Crucks and Tumuli

Almost forty years before the renowned trespass on Kinder Scout in the Peak District, the people of Bolton and its neighbouring villages were fighting for rights of access on to their own 'Kinder' – Winter Hill, a great upland lung of air, free of the cloying dirt and grime of Lancashire's mill towns. A hundred years on, people can roam freely over vast areas of the West Pennine Moors thanks to access agreements between North West Water, the local councils and farmers.

Winter Hill is now cluttered with the paraphernalia of modern man's need, but this circular walk, very much a trek through history, keeps most of that at bay before finally giving in and climbing to the top of the mountain.

The walk begins from a wooded car park off the Horwich to Rivington road through Lever Park, on the outskirts of Horwich, and not far from Lower Rivington Reservoir, which will grace the early part of the day.

Leave the car park by a path into woodland at the opposite side from the road. Ignoring a side track, keep on until you arrive within a few strides of an obviously more substantial track that leads, left, to a replica of Liverpool Castle. You may join this track, if you wish,

Rivington Pike from Lever Park

and proceed directly to the castle, but by staying on your original path, you can swing left, staying in the woodland as long as possible, and following a pleasant path that soon descends to the shores of the reservoir. By following this, you eventually arrive at the rear of the castle, perched heroically on a small rise, known as Coblowe.

The castle is a folly, a replica of the ruined Liverpool Castle as it stood after the Civil War (1642-49). It was built by the soap manufacturer and great industrialist W. H. Lever following his acquisition of the Rivington Hall estate in 1900, much of which now forms Lever Park, and a lasting monument to his name. The re-creation of the castle was begun in 1912, but suffered from limited finances; work ceased altogether when Lever died in 1925. Restoration work in recent years has been funded entirely by North West Water, which owns almost half of the land in the West Pennine Moors, and encourages visitors to view the castle.

Beyond the castle, keep with a shoreline path until forced inland, but generally staying as close to the reservoir as you can, following a broad, substantial footpath. With a certain amount of to-ing and fro-ing the path reaches a point not far from a car park serving the Great House Barn, often referred to as the Lower, or Little, Barn, to which you should direct yourself. Now an information centre and café, the barn is a fascinating construction, formed of large oak crucks, each side being taken from the same tree. This type of building frame has been in use since the earliest times until the late 17th century. It is worth noting, too, that the café is open every day of the year except Christmas Day, a sterling service that deserves support. Do this walk in winter, it is superb.

From the barn cross the road and walk up the long driveway to Rivington Hall, the late-Georgian home of the Breres family, constructed in 1780 and replacing a Tudor building. The site is mentioned in the Domesday Book, and is thought to have been the location of a Saxon manor.

Behind the house stands Rivington Hall Barn, now used for a host of social functions, but originally intended for agricultural use. No one seems sure when the barn was built, though dates ranging from 800 to 1300 have been suggested, making the structure more than a thousand years old. Dating difficulties are compounded by restoration work carried out by Viscount Leverhulme between 1900 and 1910.

Go behind the barn, following a part-tarmac track, and then immediately left on a broad, stony track to a gate. Keep ahead, and at a bend (to the right), leave the track, swinging up, left and sharply right to a stile over a fence. Follow the ensuing footpath over two more stiles to the end of a tarmac cul-de-sac and parking area, reached from the Rivington to Belmont road.

From the road end your objective is the prominent tower-like building on the skyline. To reach it, go through another gate/stile combination branching right, though a second track on the left will serve just as well, and is a little less steep. A short way along the lower track, cross a stile on the left and climb steeply to the tower ahead. The path enters woodlands just below the tower, though a direct ascent may be made. The woodlands form part of Lord Leverhulme's ornamental gardens, a complex mass of drives, ter-

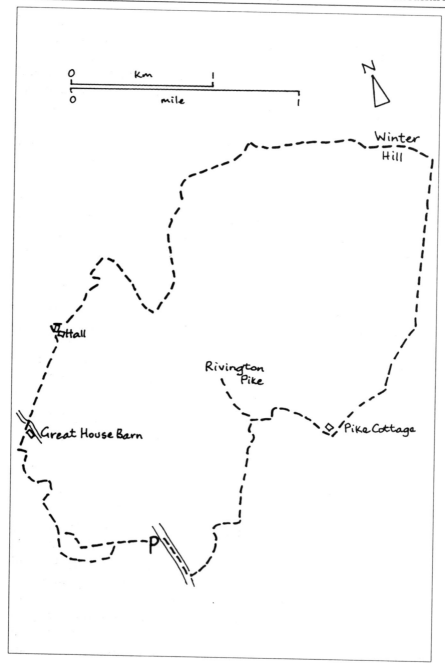

races, ponds, lawns and water gardens in the most unlikely of settings. Just after you enter the woodland a flight of steps leads up to the tower, which proves to be an attractive dovecote on the upper limit of the gardens. Many of the lodges and buildings within the gardens were demolished during the time the gardens were within the jurisdiction of Liverpool Corporation.

East of the dovecote lies Rivington Moor, which the walk now circles. Here are but a few of the Bronze Age sites to be found on the moors around Winter Hill. Three main sites are worthy of note, but the merely curious will find little on the ground to interest them. Noon Hill lies between Winter Hill and the dovecote, and here a ring cairn was excavated in the late 1950s, and is thought to date from 1100BC. Excavated at about the same time, a tumulus on Winter Hill probably dates from about 1500BC, Early Bronze Age. Later in the walk you will cross Twa Lads Moor, named after a Bronze Age twin cairn, last excavated in the seventeenth century.

By following the broad track roughly north-east you finally reach a wooden footbridge on the right, immediately below the steep face of Winter Hill. The bridge gives access to a boggy moorland path, though the worst sections have been eased by further bridges. A slithery ascent is usually the order of the day, but one with fine compensating views, especially northwards to Great Hill and the far Pennines. The path reaches the edge of the summit plateau, where a fence shepherds you upwards to be greeted by an horrendous display of man's technology. With but a moment's diversion to touch the trig pillar on the left, hasten along the tarmac road until well beyond the television relay station and its towering mast. Take care here in winter, when ice falls from the mast with lethal intent.

On the way down, just before the relay station, a metal post on the left, Scotchman's Stump, is a memorial to James Henderson, a native of Annan in Dumfriesshire (now Dumfries and Galloway), a pedlar, en route from Wigan to Belmont, who was brutally murdered on Rivington Moor in 1803.

Within a few minutes all this is past, and a steady downward plod, using the summit access road, takes you gradually away. As you follow the road down, so Rivington Pike comes into view, but do not be tempted to make a beeline for it, unless the ground is frozen solid. In normal conditions, the bog rivals Kinder and Bleaklow for its treachery.

Continue down the road until it starts to bend left, and here leave it, branching slightly right, to pursue a moorland path across the shoulder of Twa Lads Moor, from where you look out to the murky waters of distant Liverpool Bay. Eventually, the track leads you down to a rough driveway near Pike Cottage and a tea shop. Turn right here, following the drive until, at a prominent branch on the right, you can divert up to visit Rivington Pike.

This popular landmark was built in 1733 by John Andrews on the site of an ancient fire beacon. Records show that this one was certainly lit on the night of the 19th July 1588 to warn that the Spanish Armada was heading for the British coast. More recent 'firings' celebrated the Queen's Silver Jubilee in 1977, and the Royal Wedding in 1981. On a clear day, the view from Rivington Pike is outstanding, engaging not only the fells of Lakeland, but the Isle of Man and the summits of Snowdonia. From here, in particular, you can more easily pick out the Bronze Age mounds on Noon Hill, Winter Hill and Twa Lads.

Numerous ways lead down to Lever Park, and with time in hand you could launch yourself into the woodland below, searching this way and that until you finally reach the main road, there going left to return to the car park.

A more direct route involves retreating from the Pike to the rough driveway, crossing it to a gate, and descending grassy pastures, past Higher Knoll Farm, where a concrete access road is met. Follow this down, and, at a junction, go left, emerging on the main roadway close by the local grammar school. Turn right here, and in only a few minutes you return to the car park.

Walk 50: Bull Hill and the Peel Monument

Start/Finish: Car park beside the B6214, Holcombe to Haslingden road. GR.782184

Distance: 4½ miles (7.5km)

Height gain: 495ft (150m)

Walking time: 2-3 hours

Type of Walk: Easy, but muddy walking. Not suitable for misty conditions.

Map: OS Explorer 19: West Pennine Moors

Public transport: Numerous bus services operate to Ramsbottom from where the start of the walk is easily reached.

Nobbut a Spit an' a Throw

When, twenty years ago, I first tried my hand at writing about the outdoors, it was to the moors and valleys of the West Pennines that I came to learn my trade. Bound for Bull Hill one Easter Sunday, I asked the farmer from Chatterton Close how far it was. "Why, lad," he said, "it's nobbut a spit an' a throw." This walk takes you where I went that day, though the memory of it has taken me back many times since.

You start from a car park along the B6214 that runs through the village of Holcombe, situated below the frowning heights of Harcles Hill and Holcombe Moor. The village sits neatly on a natural terrace above Ramsbottom, gazing down on the Irwell valley.

Walk north along the road for a short distance until just after wooded Buckden Clough you can leave the road, on the left, to join the Rossendale Way. Far away you can pick out the great peaty domes that form the northern fringes of the Peak district.

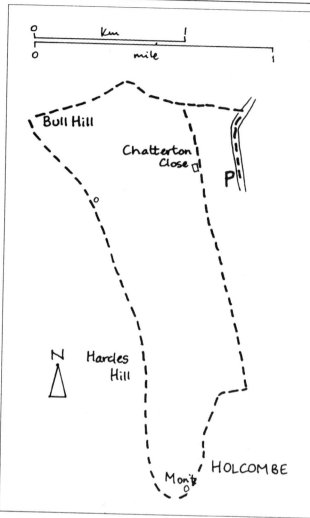

The wood-
land of Buck-
den Clough
comes to an
end quite soon,
beyond which
a broad track
branches left
past Chatterton
Close Farm.
You will return
this way, so for
the moment,
turn right to the
gate beyond the
wood and then
left, up an as-
cending track,
until you can
turn left at the
end of a wall.

Although
owned by the
National Trust,
Bull Hill, your
immediate ob-
jective, lies
within a firing
range, and
warning flags
are flown when the range is in use. The path, which continues
towards the flags, soon turns to run along the edge of the range,
safely distant from harm. Not so far away you can see the humped
form of Pendle Hill, and the long, brooding darkness of Blackstone
Edge high above unseen Hollingworth Lake.

Following the path you come to the site of the Pilgrims' Cross, a
large, four-sided monument, each side of which tells part of the

pilgrims' story. The present monument is fairly modern, but it marks the site of a cross known to have stood here in the twelfth century, and which may well have been a wayside resting place for pilgrims. No one knows what happened to the original cross. As the pilgrims discovered, this is a good place to pause for a snack, if someone else hasn't had the same idea first, or at the very least to take in the view which has now widened appreciably to include Winter Hill on the far side of these West Pennine Moors, and, on a good day, the far blue hills of North Wales.

Moving on from the Pilgrims' Cross you take a path for Holcombe Tower, and when the path forks take the right branch to the top of Harcles Hill, marked by a cairn. Once again the view has improved.

Go ahead to the next cairn, and then press on, aiming directly for Holcombe Tower, the Peel Monument, built in 1851-2 to commemorate the initiative of Sir Robert Peel in repealing the Corn Laws of yesteryear.

Peel, who originated in nearby Bury, laid the foundations for the modern police force. Indeed, when the first policemen appeared they were called, rather derisively, "peelers". Later they became known as "Roberts", and then, of course, the more familiar "bobby". Robert was what we might today refer to as one of the *nouveau riche*, and inherited considerable wealth built up by his father and grandfather. He followed his father into politics and in 1834 became Prime Minister. With the Budget deficit running at £2 million, he startled the country by instituting a tax of seven pence in the pound on incomes over £150 a year, a risky proposal since the only previous attempt to impose an income tax, by the Speaker of the House of Commons in 1450, had resulted in the proposer's murder. By 1845 the national deficit had been eradicated, and a surplus of £5 million generated. Such an achievement, certainly if extrapolated to make comparison with the crippling scale of today's Budgets, one might expect would be greeted with unanimous acclaim, but it was not so. Many die-hards disapproved of him because he had substituted Conservatism for Toryism. More was to come. Until 1846 the landed gentry had been able to protect their incomes by the Corn Laws which imposed taxes on imported foodstuffs, making them dearer than those which were produced at home. Those who supported the Corn Laws maintained that these were established to preserve the English way of life, taking the view that if cheap corn were allowed in, British farming would suffer. But the empty bellies of the country's increasing population demanded that the tax on food be repealed, an outcome that Peel initiated by introducing a Bill to repeal the old laws, succeeding in doing so only after and long and fiery debate.

From the tower which commemorates Peel's endeavours, head north-east to cross a stream and follow a path down to reach the long, straight moor road leading west of north back to Chatterton Close Farm, where, all those years ago, I was privileged to witness the Holcombe Pace Eggers performing their Easter Sunday play for the farm household.

Not far beyond the farm you rejoin your outward route, and can descend beside the wooded confines of Buckden Clough, to regain the road.

Bibliography

Countrygoers' North, Jessica Lofthouse (Robert Hale, 1965).

The Bridges of Lancashire and Yorkshire, Margaret Slack (Robert Hale, 1986)

The Buildings of England: Lancashire : 1 The Industrial and Commercial South, Nikolaus Pevsner (Penguin Books, 1969)

The Buildings of England: Lancashire: 2 The Rural North, Nikolaus Pevsner (Penguin Books, 1969)

50 Classic Walks in Lancashire, Terry Marsh (Sigma Press, 1994)

Countryside Companion, Geoffrey Young (Guild Publishing, 1985)

The Curious Traveller: Lancaster to Lakeland, Jessica Lofthouse (Robert Hale, 1956)

The Hidden Places of Lancashire, Cheshire and the Isle of Man (M&M Publishing, 3rd edition)

A History of Haigh Hall, Godfrey Talbot (Metropolitan Borough of Wigan, Booklet 2)

The Lake Counties: The King's England, Arthur Mee (Hodder and Stoughton, 1937-1969)

Lancashire: The King's England, Arthur Mee (Hodder and Stoughton, 1936).

Lancashire and the Pennines, Frank Singleton (B.T. Batsford, 1952).

Lancashire Countrygoer, Jessica Lofthouse (Robert Hale, 1962).

The Lancashire Village Book, Lancashire Federation of Women's Institutes (Countryside Books, 1990).

Lancashire Villages, Jessica Lofthouse (Robert Hale, 1973).

Lancashire-Westmorland Highway, Jessica Lofthouse (Robert Hale, 1953)

The Place Names of Lancashire, David Mills (B.T. Batsford, 1976).

Portrait of Lancashire, Jessica Lofthouse (Robert Hale, 2nd ed., 1973).

Rufford Old Hall: Lancashire (The National Trust, 1991)

The Shell Book of English Villages, John Hadfield, ed. (Michael Joseph, 1980)

South Pennines, John Gillham (Dalesman, 1996)

Traditions of Lancashire, Vol 1, John Roby (George Routledge, 1892).

Traditions of Lancashire, Second Series, Vol 2, John Roby (Frederick Warne, 1930).

A Traveller's History of England, Christopher Daniell (Windrush Press, Gloucestershire, 3rd ed 1996)

The Trials of the Lancashire Witches, E. Peel and P. Southern (David and Charles, 1969)

Also by Terry Marsh:

50 CLASSIC WALKS IN THE PENNINES

This wide-ranging book includes the Cheviots, Howgills, Yorkshire Dales and the Peak District, plus less-frequented places such as the Forest of Bowland and the South Pennines.   £8.95

More books about Lancashire:

EAST LANCASHIRE WALKS

&

WEST LANCASHIRE WALKS

These two books, both written by the 'rambling clergyman' Michael Smout are perfect for people in search of shorter walks. None is longer than six miles, but they are all packed with information and are ideal for family groups.

£6.95 each volume

BEST PUB WALKS IN LANCASHIRE

Neil Coates

Lancashire has a rich pub heritage, many excellent local breweries and a surprising variety of countryside for invigorating walks, all liable to build up a thirst! To solve the problem of where to combine the finest walks with the most notable hostelries, Neil Coates has written the most comprehensive guidebook of its type, with walks for all abilities and an excellent selection of pubs that welcome walkers.   *£6.95*

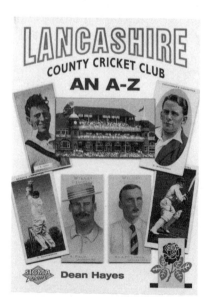

Cricket too!

LANCASHIRE COUNTY CRICKET CLUB: AN A-Z

Dean Hayes

This is the story of Lancashire cricket from the founding of the Club in 1864 right up to the present day. All the main events as well as lesser known incidents are covered as are the main controversies and the club's eternal rivalry with Yorkshire. There are over 200 entries in this A-Z, with profiles of the county's great players, anecdotes, fascinating trivia and up-to-date statistics. With its comprehensive index, this book is a must for all followers of Lancashire cricket.   *£6.95*

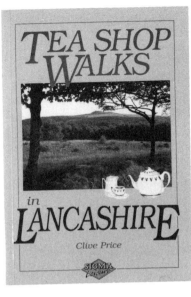

Tea Shop Walks to savour!

TEA SHOP WALKS IN LANCASHIRE

Clive Price

Clive Price's selection of 30 walks through Lancashire – taking in the best tea-rooms on the way – is a must for all locals and visitors to the county. From flagged floors to luxurious carpets, from a medieval barn to a working Post Office, the tea shops really are something special – and you can be sure the food is as good as the setting! The routes vary in length from 4 to 10 miles, so are suitable for all the family. They encompass lush riverside pastures and high, open moorlands and one enjoys the centre of Lancaster itself, with its ancient castle and Priory Church. As you explore both town and country, you can be sure of the reward of a delicious afternoon tea on the way!

In the same series:

Tea Shop Walks in the Chilterns

Tea Shop Walks in Surrey & Sussex

Tea Shop Walks in Shropshire

Tea Shop Walks in South Devon

Tea Shop Walks in the Cotswolds

Tea Shop Walks in the Lake District

Tea Shop Walks in the Peak District

Tea Shop Walks in the Yorkshire Dales

All temptingly priced at £6.95!

ORDERING INFORMATION

All of our books are available from your local bookshop. In case of difficulty, or to obtain our complete catalogue, please contact:

SIGMA LEISURE,
1 South Oak Lane, Wilmslow, Cheshire SK9 6AR
Phone: 01625-531035   Fax: 01625-536800
E-mail: sigma.press@zetnet.co.uk

ACCESS and VISA orders welcome.

Please add £2 p&p to all orders.

Free Catalogue on request.

Or visit us on the web -
http://www.sigmapress.co.uk

(The web site generally contains more comprehensive information than our printed catalogue and is updated more frequently)